THE NEWEST RUSSELL HOBBS SLOW COOKER COOKBOOK

1200 Days Simple and Delicious Slow Cooker Recipes for Busy Weeknight Meals

TABLE OF CONTENTS

MEAT RECIPES 34

FISH AND SEAFOOD RECIPES 47

DESSERT RECIPES 51

SOUPS AND STEWS RECIPES 62

SNACKS AND APPETIZERS RECIPES............76

VEGETABLES & VEGETARIAN RECIPES 89

OTHER FAVORITE RECIPES 102

INTRODUCTION

A slow cooker is an electric appliance that can cook food slowly over a period of time, usually 2 to 12 hours. To use a slow cooker, food is placed in a stoneware insert inside the slow cooker base. Heat is distributed from both the bottom and sides of the cooking vessel. You should always cook with the slow cooker lid on, so that the heat remains trapped inside the slow cooker to cook your meal.

CROCKPOT SIZES : If you are cooking for a family, I recommend a 5 or 6 quart slow cooker. Most of the slow cooker recipes that you find are tested in a 5 or 6 quart cooker. This inexpensive slow cooker is similar to the one I use. If you are cooking for one or two, a small slow cooker, such as 3 quart or 4 quart, may be ideal for you. You can halve recipes and cook them in a smaller slow cooker, but you may need to decrease the cook time a little.

COOKING TIPS

Always cook with the slow cooker lid on. This will ensure that the heat stays in and the cooking temperature is maintained. My slow cooker lid has clips on each side to seal it on tight if you need to transport food to potlucks and family dinners.Do not open your slow cooker during the cook time unless directed by the recipe. Each time you open your slow cooker, heat escapes and the cook time will be extended by about 30 minutes. You may remove the lid to check if your meal is done during the last hour or so of cooking.Avoid overfilling your slow cooker. A general rule is that it should not be more than 3/4 full. Try to fill your slow cooker at least 1/2 full to help food cook evenly.The less full your slow cooker is, the faster it will cook. For example, if you are making crockpot shredded chicken, two chicken breasts will cook faster than six chicken breasts.If you are cooking for one or two, you can halve most slow cooker recipes. You may need to reduce the cook time a little. You can double slow cooker recipes as long as they will fit in your slow cooker without filling it more than 3/4 full. If your slow cooker is very full you may have to increase the cook time.This might seem obvious, but always make sure to plug in and turn on your slow cooker after adding your ingredients. I've made the mistake of forgetting to start mine and it's a real bummer to have to throw away food because of food safety concerns.

INGREDIENT PLACEMENT

Put tougher cuts of meat and heartier vegetables, such as beef and root vegetables, in your slow cooker first. This way, they will be on the bottom and closer to the heat source. More delicate foods, such as broccoli, should go on top.Some recipes call for adding ingredients with quick cooking times, such as pasta, near the end of the cook time. Others call for thickening a sauce on the high setting after the rest of the cooking is done. If a recipe says to cook on high for 10 minutes to cook pasta or thicken a sauce, the actual cook time will depend on your particular slow cooker. It will also depend on whether your slow cooker was already cooking on the high setting or was on the low setting. If you switch from low to high, it will take additional time to reach high heat.

LOW VS HIGH COOK SETTINGS

Most slow cooker recipes will take about twice as long to cook on the low setting as the high setting. In general, low is about 200° F and high is about 300° F. The crock pot temperature may vary a bit between different slow cookers.For many foods, the low setting will give you better texture and flavor. That's the beauty of a slow cooker – cooking low and slow really develops the flavors of your meal. With that being said, I recommend choosing whether to use the low or high setting based on your schedule and what time of day you are able to start your slow cooker. Many recipes will include the cook times for both low and high.Many slow cooker recipe cook times are flexible so you can cook them longer on the low setting if you are out of the house for the day. This is true for most soups andstews, for example. However, for other recipes that include boneless chicken breasts, rice, pasta, or vegetables that fall apart (for example broccoli or zucchini), extra cook time may make them mushy or the meat tough.USDA

Food Safety Guidelines for slow cookers state to always thaw meat or poultry before putting it in your slow cooker. Since a slow cooker heats up slowly, frozen meats may stay in a temperature range (40-140 degrees F) that allows bacteria to grow for too long.For food safety, you never want to do a delayed start with a programmable slow cooker. After cooking, it is okay to set your slow cooker to switch tokeep warm. The keep warm setting is designed to keep food at a safe temperature until you eat it. Depending on your slow cooker, keep warm may continue to cook your food. I err on the side of caution and don't use keep warm for more than 2 hours, but many say you can safely leave it on warm for up to 4 hours (some dishes may be overcooked).A general rule of thumb is that foods should be refrigerated within 2 hours after they finish cooking.You can do a simple test to see if your slow cooker is working properly. Fill your slow cooker halfway full with cool water. Turn the slow cooker on the low setting and "cook" the water for 8 hours on low (do not remove the lid during this time). After 8 hours, take off the lid and immediately check the water temperature using an instant read thermometer. The water should be 185° F. If the water temperature is lower, your slow cooker may not be heating properly. If the water is hotter than 185° F your slow cooker may cook hotter than average, so you may need to reduce the cook time a bit when you follow a recipe.

PREPPING MEALS AHEAD FOR SLOW COOKING

You can do some of the prep work the evening before you plan to cook a slow cooker recipe. You can chop vegetables, cut up meat, and make sauces.

Whenever you prep ingredients ahead of time for slow cooking, store them in a bowl, covered, in your refrigerator. Transfer the food to your slow cooker insert when you are ready to start cooking.

It is not recommended that you refrigerate the ingredients that you have prepped in your slow cooker insert. Cooking in a cold insert is a food safety issue because it may take too long to heat up. Some inserts may also crack if exposed to abrupt temperature changes. With that being said, many people do store prepped ingredients in their insert in the refrigerator so it's up to you to decide what you are comfortable with.

Freezer to slow cooker meals are a great make ahead option.

HOW TO GET THE BEST FLAVOR FROM SLOW COOKER RECIPES

Brown ground meat on the stove before adding it to your slow cooker. This gives the best flavor and prevents an oily end result.For other meats, browning adds flavor but can often be skipped in the interest of time. Sautéing vegetables on the stove will also add flavor. Some foods, especially onions and fresh garlic, have better flavor after a quick sauté on the stove.When cooking meat, trim excess fat before cooking to keep the fat from ending up in your sauce. After cooking, you can let the food rest for 5 to 10 minutes and then skim off excess fat.

Be careful to not overcook meats that tend to dry out easily, such as boneless chicken breasts. Use an instant read thermometer to check the internal temperature of the chicken. As soon as it reaches 165° F at the thickest part, chicken is done.Fresh citrus (zest or juice) and fresh herbs brighten up the flavor of slow cooked food. Add them after cooking to preserve their flavor.While most fresh herbs should be added after cooking, there are a few heartier herbs, such as rosemary and thyme, that you may add before cooking.

TAKING CARE OF YOUR SLOW COOKER

Metal utensils can scratch the ceramic or stoneware insert of your slow cooker. Instead, use a wood or nylon serving spoon.When you finish eating your meal, transfer the leftovers to a storage container. Immediately give your slow cooker insert a quick rinse with hot water and then fill it with hot soapy water. Let it sit for a few minutes and it will wash easily.Slow cooker liners are a convenient option for those who find washing their slow cooker difficult.Stoneware inserts can crack if exposed to abrupt temperature changes. Do not refrigerate your insert before use or fill it with cold water right after cooking.

BREAKFAST AND BRUNCH RECIPES

Hawaiian Pulled Pork Sandwiches

Servings: 4
Cooking Time: 8 Hours

Ingredients:

- 1 packet teriyaki marinade (recommended: McCormick Grill Mates)
- 1 tablespoon paprika
- 1 teaspoon fresh ground pepper
- 3 1/2 pounds pork shoulder
- 1/2 cup chicken broth
- 1/2 cup brown sugar
- 1/4 cup soy sauce
- 1 cup chili sauce
- One 6-ounce can pineapple juice
- 1 medium onion, chopped
- 2 carrots, chopped
- 8 hamburger rolls
- Hawaiian Sauce:
- 2 tablespoon canola oil
- 1 tablespoon ginger, chopped
- 2 teaspoons garlic, chopped

Directions:

1. In small bowl, combine teriyaki mix, paprika and pepper.
2. Coat the pork the with rub mixture, patting until all rub is used. Set aside.
3. In a bowl whisk together the chicken broth, brown sugar, soy sauce, chili sauce and pineapple juice. Set aside.
4. Put the chopped onions and carrots in a 5-quart slow cooker. Place the pork on top of the carrots and onions and pour half of the pineapple juice mixture over pork. Reserve remainder for Hawaiian sauce. Cover and cook on low for 7 to 8 hours. The meat should fall apart easily. Remove the roast

from the slow cooker to a cutting board. Using 2 forks carefully pull the meat into shreds.
5. Hawaiian Sauce:
6. In a medium pot heat the oil over medium heat. Add garlic and ginger and saute until soft, about 2 minutes. Add the remaining pineapple juice mixture, bring to a boil, then reduce heat and simmer for 10 minutes. Remove from heat and set aside.
7. Serve the pork on rolls drizzled with the Hawaiian sauce or on the side for dipping.

Slow Cooker Horseradish Beef Sandwiches

Servings: 8
Cooking Time: 9 Hours

Ingredients:

- 3-4 lbs. beef chuck roast
- 1 oz. Lipton onion soup mix
- 6 garlic cloves peeled and left whole
- 3 Tbsp. Worcestershire sauce.
- ½ tsp. black pepper
- 15 oz. can beef broth
- Horseradish Sauce:
- 1 cup sour cream
- 1 Tbsp. milk or buttermilk
- 2 Tbsp. cream horseradish
- ½ tsp. salt
- 1 tsp. Worcestershire sauce

Directions:

1. Add the chuck roast to the slow cooker.
2. Sprinkle over the onion soup mix.
3. Add the garlic cloves on top of the roast.
4. Pour over the beef broth and Worcestershire sauce.
5. Cook on LOW for 9 hours.
6. While the roast is cooking, make the horseradish sauce by adding the horseradish ingredients in a

small bowl and mixing with a spoon. Refrigerate until ready to serve.

7. When the cooking time is up, shred the meat with 2 forks and discard any fat. You can do this right in the slow cooker or on a plate.

8. Toast the buns if desired. Strain the meat and place on the buns. Add the horseradish sauce on top of the meat.

NOTES

Add any remaining beef to an airtight container and store in the fridge for up to 4 days. If you're serving this for a potluck, you can cover it with the Slow Cooker top or with a piece of plastic wrap.

If you don't like the spiciness of the horseradish, use less and taste as you add it.

French bread, hoagie rolls or ciabatta rolls can be used instead of hamburger buns.

Pressure-cooker Philly Cheesesteak Sandwiches

Servings: 8
Cooking Time: 15 Minutes

Ingredients:

- 1 beef top sirloin steak (3 pounds), thinly sliced
- 2 large onions, cut into 1/2-inch strips
- 1 can (10-1/2 ounces) condensed French onion soup, undiluted
- 2 garlic cloves, minced
- 1 package Italian salad dressing mix
- 2 teaspoons beef base
- 1/2 teaspoon pepper
- 2 large red or green peppers, cut into 1/2-inch strips
- 1/2 cup pickled pepper rings
- 8 hoagie buns or French rolls, split
- 8 slices provolone cheese

Directions:

1. Combine the first 7 ingredients in a 6-qt. electric pressure cooker. Lock lid; close pressure-release valve. Adjust to pressure-cook on high for 10 minutes. Quick-release pressure. Add peppers and pepper rings. Lock lid; close pressure-release valve. Adjust to pressure-cook on high for an additional 5 minutes. Let pressure release naturally for 10 minutes; quick-release any remaining pressure.

2. Place bun bottoms on ungreased baking sheets, cut sides up. Using tongs, place beef, vegetables and cheese on bun bottoms. Broil 3-4 in. from heat until cheese is melted, 1-2 minutes. Add bun tops; serve with cooking juices.

3. Slow-cooker option: Combine the first 7 ingredients in a 4- or 5-qt. slow cooker. Cook, covered, on low 6 hours. Stir in peppers and pepper rings; cook, covered, 1-2 hours or until meat is tender.

4. Place bun bottoms on ungreased baking sheets, cut sides up. Using tongs, place beef, vegetables and cheese on bun bottoms. Broil 3-4 in. from heat until cheese is melted, 1-2 minutes. Add bun tops; serve with cooking juices.

Slow Cooker Chicken Parmesan Sandwiches

Servings: 8

Ingredients:

- 3 lbs. boneless skinless chicken breasts
- 1 tsp. salt
- 1/2 tsp. pepper
- 2 tsp. Italian Seasoning
- 1 tsp. garlic powder
- 24 oz. Marinara Sauce (I use Rao's Brand)
- 2 Tbsp. Parmesan cheese
- For serving:
- Ciabatta rolls or hamburger buns.
- Mozzarella cheese slices

Directions:

1. Add the chicken breasts to the slow cooker.

2. Sprinkle the chicken with the salt, pepper, Italian seasoning and garlic powder.

3. Pour over the marinara sauce. Sprinkle over the parmesan cheese.

4. Place the lid on the slow cooker and cook on LOW for 6 hours.

5. Shred the chicken with two forks.
6. Toast the buns and top with the shredded chicken and mozzarella cheese.

Slow-cooker Bbq Ham Sandwiches

Servings: 16
Cooking Time: 2 Hours

Ingredients:

- 3 cups ketchup
- 3/4 cup chopped onion
- 3/4 cup chopped green pepper
- 3/4 cup packed brown sugar
- 1/2 cup lemon juice
- 1/3 cup Worcestershire sauce
- 1 tablespoon prepared mustard
- 1-1/4 teaspoons ground allspice
- 1-1/2 teaspoons liquid smoke, optional
- 3 pounds thinly sliced deli ham
- 16 kaiser or ciabatta rolls, split
- Sliced pepperoncini, optional

Directions:

1. In a large saucepan, combine the first 8 ingredients; if desired, stir in liquid smoke. Bring to a boil over medium-high heat. Reduce heat; simmer, uncovered, 5 minutes, stirring occasionally.
2. Place ham in a 5- or 6-qt. slow cooker. Add sauce; stir gently to combine. Cook, covered, on low 2-3 hours or until heated through. Serve on rolls. Top with pepperoncini if desired.

Fabulous Fajitas

Servings: 8
Cooking Time: 3 Hours

Ingredients:

- 1-1/2 pounds beef top sirloin steak, cut into thin strips
- 2 tablespoons canola oil
- 2 tablespoons lemon juice
- 1 garlic clove, minced
- 1-1/2 teaspoons ground cumin
- 1 teaspoon seasoned salt
- 1/2 teaspoon chili powder
- 1/4 to 1/2 teaspoon crushed red pepper flakes
- 1 large sweet red pepper, julienned
- 1 large onion, julienned
- 8 mini flour tortillas (5 inches)
- Optional toppings: shredded cheddar cheese, fresh cilantro leaves, sliced jalapeno pepper and avocado

Directions:

1. In a large skillet, brown steak in oil over medium heat. Place steak and drippings in a 3-qt. slow cooker. Stir in the lemon juice, garlic, cumin, salt, chili powder and red pepper flakes.
2. Cover and cook on high until meat is almost tender, 2 hours. Add red pepper and onion; cover and cook until meat and vegetables are tender, 1 hour.
3. Warm tortillas according to package directions; spoon beef and vegetables down the center. Top as desired.

Vegan Banana Bread

Servings: 8-10
Cooking Time: 40 Minutes

Ingredients:

- 3 large black bananas
- 75ml vegetable oil or sunflower oil, plus extra for the tin
- 100g brown sugar
- 225g plain flour (or use self-raising flour and reduce the baking powder to 2 heaped tsp)
- 3 heaped tsp baking powder
- 3 tsp cinnamon or mixed spice
- 50g dried fruit or nuts (optional)

Directions:

1. Heat oven to 200C/180C fan/gas 6. Mash 3 large black peeled bananas with a fork, then mix well with 75g vegetable or sunflower oil and 100g brown sugar.

2. Add 225g plain flour, 3 heaped tsp baking powder and 3 tsp cinnamon or mixed spice, and combine well. Add 50g dried fruit or nuts, if using.
3. Bake in an oiled, lined 2lb loaf tin for 20 minutes. Check and cover with foil if the cake is browning.
4. Bake for another 20 minutes, or until a skewer comes out clean.
5. Allow to cool a little before slicing. It's delicious freshly baked, but develops a lovely gooey quality the day after.

Chorizo & Mozzarella Gnocchi Bake

Servings: 6
Cooking Time: 25 Minutes

Ingredients:
- 1 tbsp olive oil
- 1 onion, finely chopped
- 2 garlic cloves, crushed
- 120g chorizo, diced
- 2 x 400g cans chopped tomatoes
- 1 tsp caster sugar
- 600g fresh gnocchi
- 125g mozzarella ball, cut into chunks
- small bunch of basil, torn
- green salad, to serve

Directions:
1. Heat the oil in a medium pan over a medium heat. Fry the onion and garlic for 8-10 mins until soft. Add the chorizo and fry for 5 mins more. Tip in the tomatoes and sugar, and season. Bring to a simmer, then add the gnocchi and cook for 8 mins, stirring often, until soft. Heat the grill to high.
2. Stir ¾ of the mozzarella and most of the basil through the gnocchi. Divide the mixture between six ovenproof ramekins, or put in one baking dish. Top with the remaining mozzarella, then grill for 3 mins, or until the cheese is melted and golden. Season, scatter over the remaining basil and serve with green salad.

Slow-cooker Apple Cinnamon French Toast

Servings: 6
Cooking Time: 3 Hours

Ingredients:
- 300g brioche, cut into 2cm pieces
- 2 granny smith apples, cored, chopped
- 235g (1 cup) walnuts, coarsely chopped
- 2 tsp ground cinnamon
- 80g (1/2 cup, lightly packed) brown sugar
- 8 eggs
- 500ml (2 cups) milk
- 1 tsp vanilla extract
- Icing sugar, to dust
- Double cream, to serve
- Maple syrup, to drizzle

Directions:
1. Preheat grill on medium. Place brioche, in a single layer, on a baking tray and grill, turning occasionally, for 4 minutes or until golden.
2. Place the apple, walnut, sugar and cinnamon in a bowl and stir to combine. In a separate bowl, whisk together the eggs, milk and vanilla.
3. Lightly grease a square 17cm, 1.75L (7 cup) glass or ceramic baking dish with spray oil. Place half the bread in the dish. Sprinkle over half the apple mixture and pour over half the egg mixture. Arrange the remaining bread on top. Sprinkle with the remaining apple mixture and pour over the remaining egg mixture.
4. Place a wire trivet or rack in the base of a 5L slow cooker. Add enough water to come just to the top of the trivet. Place the baking dish on rack. Cook on low for 2 1/2-3 hours or until just set. Dust with icing sugar and top with a dollop of double cream. Drizzle with maple syrup to serve.

Cottage Pie

Servings: 10
Cooking Time: 1 Hours And 50 Minutes

Ingredients:

- 3 tbsp olive oil
- 1¼kg beef mince
- 2 onions, finely chopped
- 3 carrots, chopped
- 3 celery sticks, chopped
- 2 garlic cloves, finely chopped
- 3 tbsp plain flour
- 1 tbsp tomato purée
- large glass of red wine (optional)
- 850ml beef stock
- 4 tbsp Worcestershire sauce
- a few thyme sprigs
- 2 bay leaves
- For the mash
- 1.8kg potatoes, chopped
- 225ml milk
- 25g butter
- 200g strong cheddar, grated
- freshly grated nutmeg

Directions:

1. Heat 1 tbsp olive oil in a large saucepan and fry 1¼kg beef mince until browned – you may need to do this in batches. Set aside as it browns.

2. Put the other 2 tbsp olive oil into the pan, add 2 finely chopped onions, 3 chopped carrots and 3 chopped celery sticks and cook on a gentle heat until soft, about 20 mins.

3. Add 2 finely chopped garlic cloves, 3 tbsp plain flour and 1 tbsp tomato purée, increase the heat and cook for a few mins, then return the beef to the pan.

4. Pour over a large glass of red wine, if using, and boil to reduce it slightly before adding the 850ml beef stock, 4 tbsp Worcestershire sauce, a few thyme sprigs and 2 bay leaves.

5. Bring to a simmer and cook, uncovered, for 45 mins. By this time the gravy should be thick and coating the meat. Check after about 30 mins – if a lot of liquid remains, increase the heat slightly to reduce the gravy a little. Season well, then discard the bay leaves and thyme stalks.

6. Meanwhile, make the mash. In a large saucepan, cover the 1.8kg potatoes which you've peeled and chopped, in salted cold water, bring to the boil and simmer until tender.

7. Drain well, then allow to steam-dry for a few mins. Mash well with the 225ml milk, 25g butter, and three-quarters of the 200g strong cheddar cheese, then season with freshly grated nutmeg and some salt and pepper.

8. Spoon the meat into 2 ovenproof dishes. Pipe or spoon on the mash to cover. Sprinkle on the remaining cheese.

9. If eating straight away, heat oven to 220C/200C fan/gas 7 and cook for 25-30 mins, or until the topping is golden.

10. If you want to use a slow cooker, brown your mince in batches then tip into your slow cooker and stir in the vegetables, flour, purée, wine, stock, Worcestershire sauce and herbs with some seasoning. Cover and cook on High for 4-5 hours. Make the mash following the previous steps, and then oven cook in the same way to finish.

11. RECIPE TIPS

12. OUR TOP TIPS

13. To get really smooth, creamy mash, use a potato ricer or sieve.

14. To stop the mash sinking into the filling, allow the meat to cool before topping with the mashed potato.

15. Freeze in individual ovenproof dishes for an easy meal for one. For a really crisp, golden topping, flash under the grill for a few mins before serving.

16. FOOLPROOF FREEZING

17. Make sure the pie is completely cold, then cover it well with cling film and freeze. Always freeze the pie on the day that you make it. Defrost in the fridge overnight, then cook as per the recipe. Alternatively, to cook from frozen, heat oven to

180C/160C fan/gas 4, cover with foil and cook for 1½ hrs. Increase oven to 220C/200C fan/gas 7, uncover and cook for 20 mins more, until golden and bubbling.

Slow Cooker Pesto Mozzarella Pasta

Servings: 8
Cooking Time: 5hours

Ingredients:

- 1 1/2 lbs. chicken breasts (1.5-2 pounds works fine, 3 chicken breasts)
- 1/2 tsp. salt
- 1/4 tsp. pepper
- 8.1 oz. jarred pesto I used Classico (be sure to look at the ingredients if you have anyone allergic to nuts)
- 1/2 cup salted butter
- 1/2 lemon
- These items don't get added until the end
- 1 lb. dried rotini pasta
- 1/2 cup grated parmesan (I use the powdery shake bottle type)
- 2 cups shredded mozzarella
- 1/4 tsp. dried basil to garnish

Directions:

1. Add the chicken to the slow cooker. Sprinkle with the salt and pepper. Spread over the pesto, squeeze the lemon juice over the chicken. Cut the butter into slices and lay over the chicken.
2. Cover and cook on low for 5-6 hours without opening the lid during the cooking time.
3. Near the end of the cooking time, cook the pasta according to the package directions and drain well.
4. Shred the chicken with 2 forks. Add the cooked pasta and the parmesan cheese, stir everything until the pasta is coated with the buttery pesto sauce and the chicken is evenly dispersed throughout the pasta. Add the mozzarella cheese over the pasta. Cover for about 15 more minutes or until the cheese has melted.

5. Serve and enjoy!

NOTES

Can I omit the butter?

The butter is a main part of this and makes a delicious buttery pesto pasta. You can use chicken broth instead (1/2 cup) though this will be on the dry side.

Can I use chicken thighs instead?

You can use boneless skinless chicken thighs if you prefer dark meat. Though be sure to trim them well.

Variations:

Use a jar of sun-dried tomato pesto instead of basil pesto for a change

Add sliced mushrooms for added texture.

Change the pasta shape; you can use any hearty pasta shape such as bow-tie pasta or penne.

Slow Cooker Breakfast Burritos

Servings: 12
Cooking Time: 3 Hours 20 Minutes

Ingredients:

- 2 pounds bulk breakfast sausage
- 1 medium onion, finely chopped
- 1 medium bell pepper, finely chopped
- cooking spray
- 1 (16 ounce) package frozen shredded hash browns
- 2 ½ cups shredded Cheddar cheese
- 12 large eggs
- 1 cup milk
- 1 teaspoon kosher salt
- ½ teaspoon ground black pepper
- 12 (10 inch) flour tortillas, warmed

Directions:

1. Heat a large skillet over medium-high heat. Add sausage and cook, breaking it up with the back of a spoon, until lightly browned and crumbly, about 8 minutes. Add onion and bell pepper; cook until onion is softened, about 5 more minutes. Blot any excess oil in the pan with a paper towel. Continue to cook until sausage is cooked completely, 5 to 7 more minutes. Remove from the heat. (This step can be done 1 day ahead.)

2. Spray a slow cooker with cooking spray. Add sausage mixture, hash browns, and Cheddar cheese.

3. Whisk eggs, milk, salt, and pepper together in a bowl until well blended. Pour into the slow cooker and stir until evenly combined. Cook on Low 6 to 8 hours or on High for 3 to 4 hours, stirring after the first hour.

4. Serve mixture inside warmed tortillas with desired toppings.

NOTES:

This is easily adaptable! You can use Monterey Jack cheese instead of Cheddar. Or add in your favorite breakfast ingredients such as chopped ham, sliced chile peppers, or cooked bacon.

To speed up the cooking process, skip the slow cooker! Place the mixture in a large casserole dish and bake in a 350 degree F (175 degree C) oven for 60 to 70 minutes.

Bonus: This holds up well after the slow cooker is turned off so it can sit, covered, for an extra hour or two so breakfast doesn't have to be rushed!

Slow-cooker Pulled Turkey Sandwiches

Servings: 4-6
Cooking Time: 6 Hours

Ingredients:

- 1 small red onion, chopped
- 4 turkey thighs (about 4 pounds)
- 1 tablespoon chili powder
- 1 teaspoon ground cumin
- Kosher salt and freshly ground black pepper
- 1/2 cup ketchup
- 1/4 cup packed light brown sugar
- 2 tablespoons yellow mustard
- 1 tablespoon apple cider vinegar
- Serving suggestions: seeded hamburger buns, pickle slices, prepared coleslaw

Directions:

1. Spread the onions in the bottom of a 6- to 8-quart slow cooker. Rub the turkey thighs with the chili powder, cumin, 1 teaspoon salt and 1/2 teaspoon pepper and place over the onions. Stir together the ketchup, sugar and mustard and pour over the turkey. Cover and cook on low for 5 to 6 hours or on high for 3 to 4 hours. The turkey should be very tender with the meat falling off the bones.

2. Uncover and stir. Let cool for 10 minutes. Using two forks, shred the turkey meat, discarding the bones. Stir in the vinegar and season to taste with salt and pepper. Serve on hamburger buns with pickles and/or coleslaw if desired.

3. Cook's Note

4. Choose the higher setting (and shorting cooking time) if it's more convenient for your day.

Raspberry Coconut French Toast Slow-cooker Style

Servings: 12
Cooking Time: 2-3/4 Hours

Ingredients:

- 6 large eggs
- 1-1/2 cups refrigerated sweetened coconut milk
- 1 teaspoon vanilla extract
- 1 loaf (1 pound) French bread, cubed
- 1 package (8 ounces) cream cheese, cubed
- 2/3 cup seedless raspberry jam
- 1/2 cup sweetened shredded coconut
- Whipped cream, fresh raspberries and toasted sweetened shredded coconut

Directions:

1. In a large bowl, whisk eggs, coconut milk and vanilla until blended. Place half of the bread in a greased 5- or 6-qt. slow cooker; layer with half of the cream cheese, jam, coconut and egg mixture. Repeat layers. Refrigerate, covered, overnight.

2. Cook, covered, on low 2-3/4 to 3-1/4 hours or until a knife inserted in the center comes out clean. Serve warm with whipped cream, raspberries and toasted coconut.

Slow Cooker Veggie Omelette

Servings: 8
Cooking Time: 2 Hours

Ingredients:

- 8 large eggs
- 1/2 cup milk or Half & Half
- 1/4 cup grated parmesan cheese
- salt, to taste
- fresh ground pepper, to taste
- 1/2 tablespoon dried Italian Seasoning
- 1/2 teaspoon garlic powder, or to taste
- 1/2 teaspoon chili powder, or to taste
- 1 cup broccoli florets
- 1 small red bell pepper, diced
- 1 small yellow onion, finely chopped
- 2 cloves garlic, minced
- FOR GARNISH
- 1 cup shredded cheddar cheese
- cooked diced red peppers or diced tomatoes, optional
- finely diced onions, optional
- chopped fresh parsley, optional

Directions:

1. Lightly grease the inside of the slow cooker/Slow Cooker with cooking spray; set aside.
2. In a large mixing bowl combine eggs, milk, parmesan, salt, black pepper, Italian Seasoning, garlic powder and chili powder; using a whisk, beat the egg mixture until thoroughly combined.
3. Add broccoli florets, diced peppers, chopped onions, and garlic to the insert of your slow cooker; stir in the prepared egg-mixture.
4. Cover and cook on HIGH for 2 hours. Start checking at 1 hour 30 minutes for doneness. Omelette is done when eggs are set. You can also cook it on LOW for 3 to 3.5 hours.
5. Sprinkle with cheese and cover; let stand 2 to 3 minutes or until cheese is melted.
6. Turn off the slow cooker.
7. Optional: Garnish with chopped peppers, tomatoes, chopped onions and fresh parsley.
8. Cut the omelette into 8 pieces and serve.

Slow Cooker Kung Pao Chicken Noodles

Servings: 4
Cooking Time: 3hours

Ingredients:

- 600g chicken thigh fillets, quartered
- 2 x 145g packets Lee Kum Kee Ready Sauce for Kung Pao Chicken
- 1 small fresh red chilli, deseeded, finely chopped
- 2 carrots, peeled, halved lengthways, thinly sliced diagonally
- 1 red capsicum, deseeded, thinly sliced
- 1 yellow capsicum, deseeded, thinly sliced
- 125g snow peas, trimmed, halved diagonally
- 500g packet chow mein noodles
- 3 green shallots, cut into 4cm pieces

Directions:

1. Place chicken, sauce, chilli and 160ml (2/3 cup) water in the base of a slow cooker. Cover and cook on High for 2 hours 30 minutes or until chicken is cooked through.
2. Add carrot and capsicum to the slow cooker. Cover and cook on High for 30 minutes or until vegetables are tender, adding snow peas to the cooker in the last 15 minutes of cooking.
3. Meanwhile, cook noodles following packet directions. Drain.
4. Add noodles and shallots to the slow cooker and toss until coated. Serve.

NOTES

We used Mc Yee Noodles Chow Mein Noodles, but any chow mein noodles will work if prepared according to their packet Directions:

Slow Cooker Chicken Parmesan And Pasta

Servings: 8
Cooking Time: 6 Hours And 20 Minutes

Ingredients:

- 48 oz Ragu Pasta Sauce (two 24-oz. jars)
- 1 1/2 lbs. boneless skinless chicken breasts
- 1/2 tsp. salt
- 1/2 tsp. pepper
- 1/2 tsp. oregano (or Italian Seasoning)
- 1 lb. penne pasta cooked according to package Directions:
- 3 cups shredded mozzarella cheese
- 1/4 cup Parmesan cheese

Directions:

1. Add the chicken to a 6-quart or larger slow cooker. Sprinkle over the salt, pepper, and oregano. Pour over the pasta sauce.
2. Cover and cook on HIGH for 4 hours or LOW for 6-8 hours, without opening the lid during the cooking time.
3. When the cooking time is done, prepare the pasta on the stove-top according to the package directions.
4. While the pasta is cooking, shred the chicken with two forks. You can do this right in the slow cooker.
5. Drain the pasta very well. Add the pasta to the chicken and sauce in the slow cooker. Stir. Flatten the pasta out into an even layer. Sprinkle over the shredded mozzarella cheese and parmesan cheese. Cover for 15 more minutes, or until the cheese has melted.

NOTES

Can I use a different shape of pasta?
You can use rotini, rigatoni, bow-tie, or even spaghetti noodles in this dish. I do not recommend using egg noodles.

How to store:
Place the cooked and cooled pasta into freezer ziplock bags or plastic containers. Store in the fridge for three days or in the freezer for three months.

How to Reheat

Slow Cooker Shepherd's Pie

Servings: 4
Cooking Time: 5 Hours

Ingredients:

- 1 tbsp olive oil
- 1 onion, finely chopped
- 3-4 thyme sprigs
- 2 carrots, finely diced
- 250g lean (10%) mince lamb or beef
- 1 tbsp plain flour
- 1 tbsp tomato purée
- 400g can lentils, or white beans
- 1 tsp Worcestershire sauce
- For the topping
- 650g potatoes, peeled and cut into chunks
- 250g sweet potatoes, peeled and cut into chunks
- 2 tbsp half-fat crème fraîche

Directions:

1. Heat the slow cooker if necessary. Heat the oil in a large frying pan. Tip the onions and thyme sprigs and fry for 2-3 mins. Then add the carrots and fry together, stirring occasionally until the vegetables start to brown. Stir in the mince and fry for 1-2 mins until no longer pink. Stir in the flour then cook for another 1-2 mins. Stir in the tomato purée and lentils and season with pepper and the Worcestershire sauce, adding a splash of water if you think the mixture is too dry. Scrape everything into the slow cooker.
2. Meanwhile cook both lots of potatoes in simmering water for 12-13 minutes or until they are cooked through. Drain well and then mash with the crème fraîche. Spoon this on top of the mince mixture and cook on Low for 5 hours - the mixture should be bubbling at the sides when it is ready. Crisp up the potato topping under the grill if you like.

Slow Cooker Chicken Fajitas Recipe

Servings: 5
Cooking Time: 4 Hours

Ingredients:

- 1 red bell pepper sliced
- 1 green bell pepper sliced
- 1 small white onion sliced
- 2 lbs. chicken breast tenderloins
- 1/2 tsp. salt
- 1/4 tsp. black pepper
- 1 tsp. chili powder
- 2 tsp. minced garlic (or 1 tsp. dried garlic powder)
- 1/8 cup chopped cilantro
- 1 small lime
- 2 Tbsp. canola or vegetable oil
- For serving:
- warmed tortillas corn or flour
- shredded cheese
- avocado
- sour cream

Directions:

1. Add the bell peppers and onions to the slow cooker. Toss them together with clean hands. Lay over the chicken breast tenderloins. Sprinkle over the salt, pepper, chili powder, garlic, and cilantro. Cut the lime in half and squeeze the juices over everything in the slow cooker. Drizzle over the oil next.
2. Place the lid on the slow cooker and cook on HIGH for 4 hours or LOW for 6-8. Do not open the lid during the cooking time.
3. Serve on warmed tortillas with desired toppings. Enjoy!

NOTES

Can I make this into a freezer meal?

Yes, you can make this into a freezer meal to cook later. Add all the ingredients to a ziplock bag. Freeze for up to three months. When you are ready to make it, thaw, and continue with

I like my peppers firm; when should I add them?

Add the pepper during the last hour of cooking if you like them firmer. I recommend adding the onions initially; they take much longer to soften.

How can I make this spicy?

Add 1-2 minced jalapenos along with the other seasonings if you want a spicy fajita.

How to store:

Place the chicken and vegetables in airtight containers. You can keep it in the fridge for up to three days or the freezer for three months.

Slow-cooker Breakfast Casserole

Servings: 8

Ingredients:

- 1 lb. bacon
- Cooking spray
- 12 large eggs
- 1 c. whole milk
- 1/2 tsp. garlic powder
- Kosher salt
- Freshly ground black pepper
- 1 1/2 lb. frozen hash browns
- 1 medium onion, chopped
- 2 c. shredded cheddar
- Freshly chopped chives, for garnish

Directions:

1. In a large skillet over medium heat, cook bacon until crispy, 8 minutes. Drain on a paper towel-lined plate, then chop.
2. Grease inside of your slow cooker with cooking spray. In a large bowl, whisk together eggs and milk and season with garlic powder, salt, and pepper.
3. In the slow cooker, layer half the hash browns, cooked bacon, onion, and cheese. Repeat layers, then pour over whisked eggs.
4. Cover and cook on low until eggs are fluffy and set, about 6 hours.
5. Garnish with green onions before serving.

Chicken Alfredo Sandwich

Servings: 6
Cooking Time: 4 Hours

Ingredients:

- 3 pounds boneless, skinless chicken breasts (about 5-6 breasts)
- 1½ cups Alfredo sauce store-bought or homemade
- ¼ cup chopped fresh basil
- ¼ cup chopped onion
- 1 teaspoon garlic powder
- ¼ cup finely chopped sun-dried tomatoes drained and rinsed if packed in oil
- ½ cup freshly grated Parmesan cheese
- Kosher salt and freshly ground black pepper to taste
- 6 hamburger buns for serving

Directions:

1. Place all ingredients except the chicken in a slow cooker and stir to combine.
2. 1½ cups Alfredo sauce,¼ cup chopped fresh basil,¼ cup chopped onion,1 teaspoon garlic powder,¼ cup finely chopped sun-dried tomatoes,½ cup freshly grated Parmesan cheese,Kosher salt and freshly ground black pepper
3. Add in the chicken and coat with the sauce.
4. 3 pounds boneless, skinless chicken breasts
5. Cook on low for 6-7 hours or high for 3-4 hours, until chicken is cooked through.
6. Remove chicken from the slow cooker and use two forks to fully shred.
7. Return shredded chicken to the slow cooker and coat in the sauce.
8. To assemble the sandwiches, top with more sun dried tomatoes, shaved parmesan, and spinach.
9. 6 hamburger buns

NOTES

Storage: Store chicken Alfredo sandwiches in an airtight container in the refrigerator for up to 3 days.

Slow Cooker Spaghetti Squash And Sauce

Servings: 4
Cooking Time: 4 Hours

Ingredients:

- 1 lb. ground turkey I used 7% fat
- 1 Tbsp. cooking oil
- 3 lb. spaghetti squash
- 23.5 oz. jar marinara sauce
- 1 portabello mushroom diced
- 1 small white onion diced
- 1 garlic clove minced
- 1/2 tsp. salt
- 1/4 tsp. pepper
- 1/2 tsp. oregano
- 1/2 tsp. basil

Directions:

1. In a large pan on the stove-top set to medium-high heat, add cooking oil. Brown the turkey. Add to the slow cooker. Add the marinara sauce, mushrooms, onion, garlic, salt, pepper, oregano, and basil to the slow cooker as well. Stir.
2. Cut the spaghetti squash in half, remove the seeds with a spoon.
3. Add the squash cut side down in the slow cooker into the sauce.
4. Cover and cook on HIGH for 4 hours. Do not open the lid during the cooking time.

NOTES

I use ground turkey, though you can use ground beef, ground chicken, or ground pork.

Place the leftovers in the fridge for up to four days or freezer for up to three months.

Boston Baked Beans With Frying Pan Cornbread

Servings: 6

Cooking Time: 10hours And 10 Minutes

Ingredients:

- 1 1/2 cups (300g) dried beans (such as white or black beans)
- 1 tbsp olive oil
- 1 brown onion, finely chopped
- 2 middle bacon rashers, finely chopped
- 2 garlic cloves, crushed
- 2 tsp ground paprika
- 1 tsp ground cumin
- 2 x 400g cans diced tomatoes
- 1 tbsp Worcestershire sauce
- 1 tbsp golden syrup
- 2 tsp Dijon mustard
- Coriander leaves, to serve
- Frying pan cornbread
- 3/4 cup (110g) plain flour
- 3/4 cup (125g) cornmeal (polenta)
- 2 tsp baking powder
- 1 cup (160g) frozen corn kernels
- 1/2 cup (60g) cheddar, coarsely grated
- 1 long red chilli, seeded, finely chopped
- 1/2 cup coarsely chopped coriander
- 3/4 cup (185ml) buttermilk
- 1 Coles Brand Australian free range egg, lightly whisked
- 50g butter, melted

Directions:

1. Place the beans in a large bowl and cover with plenty of cold water. Set aside overnight to soak.
2. Heat the oil in a medium frying pan over medium heat. Add onion, bacon and garlic. Cook, stirring, for 5 mins or until onion softens. Add paprika and cumin. Cook for 1 min or until aromatic.
3. Drain the beans and place in a slow cooker. Add the onion mixture, tomato, Worcestershire sauce, golden syrup and mustard. Cook on high for 10 hours (or on low for 12 hours), or until the beans are very tender.
4. Meanwhile, to make the cornbread, preheat oven to 200C. Combine the flour, cornmeal, baking powder, corn, cheddar, chilli and coriander in a large bowl. Whisk the buttermilk, egg and butter in a jug. Add to the flour mixture and stir to combine.
5. Brush a 20cm round ovenproof frying pan with oil. Place over medium heat. Pour in the batter and use the back of a spoon to smooth the surface. Reduce heat to low. Cook, covered, for 10 mins or until almost cooked. Transfer pan to oven. Bake for 10 mins or until golden.
6. Spoon the baked beans among serving plates and sprinkle with coriander. Cut the cornbread into wedges and serve with the baked beans.

NOTES

In the oven: If you don't have a slow cooker, bake the bean mixture in a casserole dish at 160°C, stirring occasionally, for 3 hours or until very tender.

POULTRY RECIPES

Slow Cooker Cornish Game Hens And Baked Potatoes

Servings: 3
Cooking Time: 7 Hours

Ingredients:

- 3 Cornish game hens THAWED - this takes about 36 hours in the fridge
- 3 medium-sized russet potatoes washed and dried
- 1/2 lemon
- 1 tsp. sea salt (plus more for potatoes)
- 1/4 tsp. ground pepper (plus more for potatoes)
- 1/4 tsp. paprika
- 1/2 tsp. basil
- 2 Tbsp. olive oil
- Suggesting serving items:
- toppings for baked potatoes such as butter, sour cream, chives and bacon bits.

Directions:

1. NOTE - THE GAME HENS NEED TO BE THAWED COMPLETELY. This takes about 36 hours in the fridge.
2. Remove the game hens from their packaging. Rinse them under cold water to remove any debris from their insides and any stuck pieces of ice.
3. Pat the game hens dry with paper towels.
4. Add the game hens breast up to the slow cooker.
5. Squeeze the lemon over the game hens.
6. Sprinkle them with the 1 teaspoon of salt, 1/4 teaspoon of pepper, paprika and basil. Be sure to sprinkle the paprika over evenly, this will keep the hens from looking pale after cooking.
7. Add the russet potatoes on top, I tuck the potatoes in the empty spaces around the chicken. (no need to pierce the potaotes with a fork)
8. Drizzle the olive oil over the potatoes. Sprinkle the potatoes with a touch of salt and pepper.
9. Place the lid on the slow cooker.
10. Cook for 7 hours on low. DO NOT OPEN THE LID DURING THE COOKING TIME. Check to see if the chicken is cooked through and the potatoes are tender before serving. Cook for an additional hour if your potatoes aren't tender, for every slow cooker cooks slightly different.

NOTES

Cornish game hens should have an internal temperature of 165 degrees Fahrenheit. You can also tell if your hens are done if your meat is no longer pink and the juices run clear. The slow cooker usually cooks things past the point of doneness and makes for very tender chicken.

Ideally, this recipe can serve 3 people (very large servings, with possible leftovers). If you have kids to feed, there is plenty of food to share, though you will need to split the chicken and potaotes.

Do I have to thaw the game hens?

It is important to thaw the game hens before cooking. The chicken needs to be thawed to ensure they cook properly and get done at the same time as the potatoes. Be sure to plan ahead.

Can I add foil around my potatoes?

This recipe will work with or without foil. Since it works without and the potatoes don't get soggy, I skip that step.

Variations

Cajun - You can add cayenne pepper, onion and garlic powder to make this dish Cajun. Or use a cajun spice blend such as Tony Chachures Creole Blend (omit the salt from the recipe, this blend can be VERY salty).

Garlic herb - Add 2-3 cloves of minced garlic over the game hens along with the original recipe.

Barbecue - brush barbecue sauce over the done cooking game hens for a completely different meal.

Shredded Sweet Soy Chicken Breast

Servings: 4
Cooking Time: 1 Hour

Ingredients:

- Shredded Chicken
- 1 lb / 500g chicken breast (skinless, boneless pieces)
- 2 cloves of garlic , minced
- 1/2 onion , finely diced
- 1 tbsp oil (vegetable, canola, olive oil or grapeseed oil)
- 1/3 cup soy sauce (ordinary soy sauce)
- 1/3 cup white vinegar (or substitute with other vinegar except balsamic)
- 3 tbsp jam (Note 1)
- 1 tbsp black peppercorns or 1/2 tbsp ground black pepper (Note 2)
- 3/4 cups water
- Sauce Thickening
- 2 tsp cornstarch / cornflour
- 3 tsp water

Directions:

1. Slow Cooker: Place all the Shredded Chicken ingredients in the slow cooker and cook on low for 5 hours (or 2 1/2 hours on high).
2. Pressure Cooker: Place all the Shredded Chicken ingredients in the pressure cooker. Cook for 35 minutes on high.
3. Stove: Place all the Shredded Chicken ingredients in a saucepan large enough for the chicken to fit snugly in one layer. Add 1/2 cup extra water so the chicken is mostly, but not completely submerged. Cover and simmer for about 50 to 60 minutes, turning once or twice.
4. The chicken is ready when it can be easily shredded with two forks. Remove the chicken from the liquid and shred it while it is warm. Set aside and cover to keep warm.
5. Transfer the liquid from the slow cooker / pressure cooker to a saucepan and bring to simmer. (Note 3)

Reduce to around1 1/4 cups - it should only take a few minutes.
6. Mix together the Sauce Thickening ingredients and add to the saucepan. Simmer until it it thickens to a syrup consistency.
7. Toss the chicken in the sauce and serve over rice. (Note 4)

NOTES

I used blueberry jam. Blackberry or other dark ones are great but you can use any flavour at all because the jam is used as the sweetener / thickening agent for the sauce rather than flavour.

I like pops of black pepper in this. It's not that spicy because it becomes mild once cooked. But if you're making this for kids, I recommend using ground pepper.

If your slow cooker has a saute setting, you can do this in your slow cooker. If you are using a stovetop pressure cooker, you can do this in the pressure cooker. The sauce is great to use for fried rice, as is the chicken. Just stir fry onions and garlic, add diced vegetables, then day old cooked rice, the chicken and the sauce. Stir fry to heat through, then serve!

You can add extra flavourings if you want! I like to add ginger, sriracha or red pepper flakes, a dash of hoisin or oyster sauce, or sesame oil.

Freeze leftovers after cooking and tossing in sauce. To use, allow to defrost then I recommend pan frying with a bit of oil. This will revitalise it as the sauce tends to become a bit watery when it defrosts.

Slow Cooker Cheesy Buffalo Chicken Pasta

Servings: 6
Cooking Time: 5 Hours

Ingredients:

- 1 1/2 pounds boneless skinless chicken
- 3 cups chicken broth
- 1/2 cup buffalo wing sauce (1/4 cup now, 1/4 cup later)
- 1 tablespoon ranch dressing mix (packet kind)
- 1/2 teaspoon garlic powder

- 1/4 teaspoon celery salt
- 1/4 teaspoon salt
- 1/8 teaspoon pepper
- 8 ounces cream cheese
- 1 cup shredded sharp cheddar
- 1 tablespoon corn starch + 1 tablespoon water
- 16 ounces linguine noodles
- Chopped cilantro for garnish optional

Directions:

1. Place chicken, broth, 1/4 cup buffalo sauce, and seasonings in crock
2. Top with cream cheese and shredded cheese
3. Cover and cook on high for 4 hours or low for 8
4. When chicken is fully cooked remove to separate bowl and shred with two forks
5. Add remaining 1/4 cup buffalo sauce to chicken and toss to coat
6. Set aside chicken
7. Whisk together corn starch and water and add to crock
8. Use a whisk and stir until cheese and cream cheese (which were added in step 2 and should now be soft and melted) are all combined and smooth
9. Break noodles in half and place in crock
10. Top with chicken and cover
11. Turn crock on high for 30-60 minutes until noodles are fully cooked, stir 3-4 times during cooking
12. If noodles are not done you can add extra broth or water 1/4 cup at a time
13. Garnish with cilantro if desired and serve immediately

NOTES

I made this in my 5 quart crock. It wasn't full but it gave me plenty of room to stir.

Slow-cooker Chicken Breast

Servings: 3

Ingredients:

- 1 red onion, chopped
- 1 lb. baby red potatoes, quartered
- Juice of 1/2 lemon
- 3 tbsp. extra-virgin olive oil
- Kosher salt
- Freshly ground black pepper
- 1 tsp. garlic powder
- 3 boneless skinless chicken breasts (about 1 1/4 lb.)
- 1 sprig rosemary

Directions:

1. In a slow-cooker, toss onion, potatoes, and lemon juice together with olive oil. Spread into an even layer.
2. In a large bowl, stir together salt, pepper, and garlic powder. Add chicken breasts and toss to coat evenly.
3. Place chicken in a single layer above the onion mixture and top with rosemary.
4. Cook on low until chicken is cooked through and potatoes are fork-tender, 4 to 5 hours.

Saucy Chicken & Vegetables

Servings: 2
Cooking Time: 30 Minutes

Ingredients:

- 2 chicken breasts, skin on
- 1 tbsp olive oil
- 200g new potato, thinly sliced
- 500ml chicken stock
- 200g pack of mixed spring vegetables (broccoli, peas, broad beans and sliced courgette)
- 2 tbsp crème fraîche
- handful tarragon leaves, roughly chopped

Directions:

1. Fry the chicken in the oil in a wide pan for 5 mins on each side. Throw in the potatoes and stir to coat. Pour over the chicken stock, cover and simmer for

10 mins until the potatoes are almost cooked through.

2. Remove the lid and turn the heat to high. Boil the stock down until it just coats the bottom of the pan. Scatter the vegetables into the pan, cover again and cook the veg for about 3 mins.

3. Stir in the crème fraîche to make a creamy sauce, season with pepper and salt, if you want, then add the tarragon. Serve straight from the pan.

NOTES

MAKING IT TANGY

For a mustardy sauce, stir 1 tbsp of wholegrain mustard in with the crème fraîche. Use 1tbsp of dried tarragon instead of fresh.

IF YOU WANT TO USE A SLOW COOKER...

Brown the chicken, skin-side down in a frying pan for 5 mins. Turn the chicken over then throw in the potatoes and stir to coat. Spread the potatoes along the bottom of the slow cooker, sit the chicken on top, pour over 250ml stock then cover and cook on High for an hour and a half. Remove the chicken and stir in the veg. Put the chicken back on top and cook for another hour until cooked through. Stir in the crème frâiche according to step 3 and serve.

Slow Cooker Cheesy Buffalo Chicken Flautas

Servings: 5
Cooking Time: 5 Hours

Ingredients:

- 2 lbs. Boneless Skinless Chicken Breasts
- 1 cup Frank's Red Hot Buffalo Sauce
- 1 Tbsp. cornstarch
- 1/4 tsp. pepper
- 2 Tbsp. butter
- 10 8-inch flour tortillas
- 16 oz. shredded mozzarella cheese
- 2 Tbsp. melted butter this is for basting the tortillas
- Ranch or blue cheese dressing for serving

Directions:

1. Place the chicken into a 4-quart or larger slow cooker. In a small bowl, whisk together the buffalo sauce, cornstarch and pepper. Pour this mixture over the chicken. Cut the butter into 2 pieces and place on top of chicken.

2. Cover and cook on LOW for 5 hours.

3. Shred the chicken with two forks.

4. Use tongs to get the chicken out of the slow cooker, tap the tongs on the side of the slow cooker to get the excess sauce off the chicken.

5. Place about a 1/2 cup of chicken into each tortilla and top with a heaping 1/8 cup of cheese.

6. Roll up the tortillas around the filling and secure with a toothpick. Note- If your tortillas start to crack while rolling them up. Wrap them in moist paper towels (before filling them) and microwave for 25 seconds.

7. Place the flautas onto a baking pan that has been sprayed with non-stick cooking spray.

8. Baste the flautas with the melted butter.

9. Preheat the oven to 425 degrees.

10. Cook the flautas for about 7 minutes, flipping once, and cooking for an additional 7 minutes or until golden brown.

11. Remove toothpicks.

12. Serve with ranch or blue cheese dressing.

Slow Cooker Buffalo Ranch Drumsticks

Servings: 6
Cooking Time: 4 Hours

Ingredients:

- 4 lbs. chicken drumsticks
- 2 garlic cloves, minced
- 1/8 tsp. cayenne pepper
- 1/4 tsp pepper
- 1 oz. Ranch dressing mix
- 1 cup Frank's Red Hot
- 1/4 cup salted butter melted

Directions:

1. Remove the skin from the drumsticks. I do this by pulling the skin as far down as I can, then when I can pull any further I grab onto the skin with a

paper towel and the skin usually comes right off. I did have to cut the skin off of a few.

2. Place the chicken into the slow cooker. Sprinkle over the garlic, cayenne, pepper, and ranch dressing mix. Pour over the Frank's Red Hot and the melted butter. Stir.

3. Place the lid on the slow cooker, and cook on HIGH for 4 hours without opening the lid during the cooking time.

Sage Chicken Cordon Bleu

Servings: 6
Cooking Time: 40 Minutes

Ingredients:

- 6 boneless skinless chicken breast halves (4 ounces each)
- 1/2 to 3/4 teaspoon rubbed sage
- 6 slices thinly sliced deli ham
- 6 slices part-skim mozzarella cheese, halved
- 1 medium tomato, seeded and chopped
- 1/3 cup dry bread crumbs
- 2 tablespoons grated Parmesan cheese
- 2 tablespoons minced fresh parsley
- 4 tablespoons butter, divided

Directions:

1. Preheat oven to 350°. Flatten the chicken breasts with a meat mallet to 1/8-in. thickness; sprinkle with sage. Place ham, mozzarella cheese and tomato down the center of each; roll up chicken from a long side, tucking in ends. Secure with toothpicks.

2. In a shallow bowl, toss bread crumbs with Parmesan cheese and parsley. In a shallow microwave-safe dish, microwave 3 tablespoons butter until melted. Dip chicken in butter, then roll in crumb mixture. Place in a greased 11x7-in. baking dish, seam side down. Melt remaining butter; drizzle over top.

3. Bake, uncovered, until a thermometer inserted in chicken reads 165°, 40-45 minutes. Discard toothpicks before serving.

Slow Cooker Coq Au Vin

Servings: 4
Cooking Time: 4 Hours

Ingredients:

- 8 skin-on, bone-in chicken thighs
- 30g butter
- 140g smoked bacon lardons or diced smoked pancetta
- 400g pearl onions or small shallots peeled and left whole (see tip, below)
- 2 large or 4 small carrots, peeled and cut into chunks
- 2 garlic cloves, crushed
- 3 tbsp plain flour
- 1 tbsp tomato purée
- 300ml chicken stock
- 600ml red wine
- 2 bay leaves
- 1 large thyme sprig
- 300g button chestnut mushrooms, kept whole, larger ones chopped
- handful of parsley leaves, chopped (optional)
- mash or buttered tagliatelle, to serve

Directions:

1. Season the chicken. Melt half the butter in a deep frying pan or large flameproof casserole over a medium heat and cook the chicken, skin-side down, for 10 mins until deep golden. Flip to seal the fleshy side for a few minutes – you may need to do this in batches. Put in the slow cooker.

2. Tip the bacon into the same pan and fry for 5-6 mins until crisp, then add to the slow cooker. Tip the onions or shallots and carrots into the pan and fry in the bacon fat for 5 mins until starting to colour. Add the garlic, cook for 1 min more, then sprinkle over the flour and cook for 1-2 mins until you have a sandy paste. Stir through the tomato purée and cook for 2 mins more. Bring to the boil, then turn down to a simmer for 2 mins.

3. Tip the contents of the pan over the chicken. Pour the stock and wine into the pan, bring to the boil, then pour into the slow cooker. Nestle in the bay

leaves and thyme, season, then set the slow cooker on high for 3-4 hrs, 5-6 hrs on medium or 7-8 hrs on low, stirring once or twice, until the chicken is tender.

4. While the chicken cooks, heat the remaining butter in a clean pan and fry the mushrooms for 4-5 mins over a medium heat. Tip into the slow cooker about an hour before the end of cooking and stir. At this stage, the coq au vin can be cooled and kept chilled for up to three days or frozen for up to three months. Defrost and reheat in a pan over a medium heat until piping hot. Scatter over the parsley, if using, and serve with mash or buttered tagliatelle.

NOTES

Baby onions or shallots can be tricky to peel, but if you leave them soaking in boiled water for a few minutes, then drain and leave to cool, the skins just slip off.

Slow Cooker White Chicken Chili

Servings: 6

Ingredients:

* 2 1/2 c. low-sodium chicken broth
* 2 (15.5-oz.) cans white beans, drained and rinsed
* 1 1/2 lb. boneless skinless chicken breasts
* 2 (4-oz.) cans green chiles
* 1 small yellow onion, finely chopped
* 2 cloves garlic, minced
* 1 jalapeño, seeded and minced, plus more for serving
* 1 tsp. dried oregano
* 1 tsp. ground cumin
* Kosher salt
* Freshly ground black pepper
* 1 1/2 c. frozen corn
* FOR SERVING
* Sour cream
* Sliced avocado
* Thinly sliced jalapeño
* Freshly chopped cilantro
* Lime wedges

Directions:

1. Add broth, beans, chicken, green chiles, onion, garlic, jalapeño, oregano, and cumin to the bowl of your slow cooker. Season with salt and pepper and cook on high for 2 to 3 hours, until chicken is tender.

2. Remove chicken from chili and shred. Use a potato masher to gently mash about 1/3 of the beans before returning chicken to slow cooker. Stir in shredded chicken and corn and cover and season with more salt and pepper if needed. Leave slow cooker on warm until ready to serve.

3. To serve, top with sour cream, avocado, jalapeño, cilantro, and a squeeze of lime juice.

Slow-cooker Chicken Korma

Servings: 4-6

Cooking Time: 6 Hours 20 Minutes

Ingredients:

* 2 garlic cloves
* thumb-sized piece ginger, peeled
* 2 large onions, finely chopped
* 2 tbsp vegetable oil
* 6 skinless chicken breasts, cut into large chunks
* 2 tbsp tomato purée
* 1 tsp ground cumin
* 1 tsp paprika
* 1 tsp turmeric
* 1 tsp ground coriander
* ¼-½ tsp chilli powder
* 2 tsp sugar
* 300ml chicken stock
* 150ml double cream
* 6 tbsp ground almonds
* toasted flaked almonds, coriander, basmati rice and naan breads, to serve (optional)

Directions:

1. Heat the slow cooker to low. Put the garlic, ginger and onions in a small blender with a splash of water and whizz to a paste. Heat the oil in a frying pan over a medium-high heat and sear the chicken all over. Remove from the pan and set aside, then add

the onion paste. Fry over a medium heat for 10 mins until lightly golden.

2. Stir in the tomato purée, spices, 1 tsp salt and the sugar, fry for 1 min until aromatic, then put the chicken back into the pan (with any resting juices) and add the stock. Stir and bring to a simmer, then spoon into the slow cooker. Cook on low for 5-6 hrs until the chicken is tender and cooked through.

3. Stir through the cream and the ground almonds and bubble for 10 mins to reduce, if needed. Scatter with flaked almonds and coriander, if using, then serve with rice and naans, if you like.

Slow Cooker Chicken Adobo Recipe

Servings: 5
Cooking Time: 6 Hours

Ingredients:

- 5 skin-on bone-in chicken thighs
- 2 Tbsp. cooking oil
- 1/4 cup reduced sodium soy sauce regular soy sauce will work fine as well
- 1/4 cup white vinegar (can use apple cider vinegar)
- 1 cup chicken broth
- 1 cup white onion diced
- 3 garlic cloves left whole
- 3 small slices of peeled fresh ginger root (or 1/4 tsp. ground ginger)
- 2 bay leaves
- 10-15 black peppercorns (or 1/4 teaspoon ground black pepper)
- 1 bunch green onion sliced - for serving

Directions:

1. Set a large skillet over medium-high heat. When the pan is hot add enough of the oil to coat the bottom of the pan. Brown the chicken on both sides. Add the chicken to the slow cooker.

2. In a medium sized bowl whisk together the soy sauce, vinegar, chicken broth and onion. Pour this mixture over the chicken. Or you can add everything to the slow cooker without dirtying a bowl, this works fine too.

3. Add the garlic cloves, ginger slices, bay leaves and peppercorns on top of the chicken.

4. Cover and cook on LOW for 6-7 hours or HIGH 4 hours for without opening the lid during the cooking time.

5. Remove bay leaves, and garlic cloves if desired.

6. Serve chicken drizzled with plenty of the sauce out of the slow cooker and enjoy! Top with sliced green onion for flavor and texture.

NOTES

Can I use a different cut of chicken?

Yes, though bone-in dark meat works best for this recipe you can use pretty much any cut of chicken. Try to stick with around 2 pounds so there is plenty of sauce to flavor the chicken.

Drumsticks

Bone-in chicken breast

Boneless skinless thighs or breasts

Can I make this into shredded chicken?

If you desire shredded chicken, remove the chicken on a plate. Remove and discard the skin.

Shred the chicken off the bone and add back into the slow cooker with the sauce.

This shredded chicken is great over rice.

What goes good with chicken adobo?

Steamed white rice

Steamed green veggies such as asparagus, bok choy, sugar snap peas or broccoli

Cauliflower rice for if you're watching your carbs. This chicken adobo is very low in carbs!

Can I add bok choy into the slow cooker with the chicken?

Yes! Add 3-4 cups of sliced bok choy during the last 5-10 minutes of cooking time.

Bbq Chicken Sliders

Servings: 8
Cooking Time: 4 Hours

Ingredients:

- BRINE:
- 1-1/2 quarts water
- 1/4 cup packed brown sugar
- 2 tablespoons salt

- 1 tablespoon liquid smoke
- 2 garlic cloves, minced
- 1/2 teaspoon dried thyme
- SANDWICHES:
- 2 pounds boneless skinless chicken breasts
- 1/3 cup liquid smoke
- 1-1/2 cups hickory smoke-flavored barbecue sauce
- 16 slider buns or dinner rolls, split and warmed
- Deli coleslaw, optional

Directions:

1. In a large bowl, mix brine ingredients, stirring to dissolve brown sugar. Reserve 1 cup brine for cooking chicken; cover and refrigerate.
2. Place chicken in bowl with remaining brine; turn to coat chicken. Cover and refrigerate 18-24 hours, turning occasionally.
3. Remove chicken from brine and transfer to a 3-qt. slow cooker; discard brine from bowl. Add reserved 1 cup brine and 1/3 cup liquid smoke to chicken. Cook, covered, on low 4-5 hours or until chicken is tender.
4. Remove chicken; cool slightly. Discard cooking juices. Shred chicken with 2 forks and return to slow cooker. Stir in barbecue sauce; heat through. Serve on buns, with coleslaw if desired.

Slow Cooker Chipotle Chicken

Servings: 6
Cooking Time: 6 Hours 20 Minutes

Ingredients:

- 1 tbsp. vegetable oil
- 2 red onions, sliced
- 3 garlic cloves, crushed
- 1 tsp. smoked paprika
- 2 tsp. ground coriander
- 2 tbsp. tomato purée
- 1 -2tbsp chipotle paste, to taste
- 2 mixed coloured peppers, finely sliced
- 400 g tin black beans, drained and rinsed
- 400 g tin chopped tomatoes
- 4 tbsp. chicken stock or water
- 800 g chicken thigh fillets

- Juice 2 limes
- Large handful fresh coriander, roughly chopped (optional)

Directions:

1. Heat oil in a frying pan over medium heat. Add the onions with a large pinch of salt and cook for 15min, until beginning to soften. Add the garlic and cook for 2min, until fragrant.
2. Add the paprika, ground coriander, tomato purée and chipotle paste and fry for a further 1min.
3. Scrape onion mixture into the bowl of the slow cooker and stir in the peppers, beans, tomatoes, stock or water and some seasoning. Season the chicken thigh fillets and place on top of the tomato mixture in the slow cooker.
4. Cover with the lid and cook on low for 6hr, until the chicken is tender enough to pull apart.
5. Shred the chicken with two forks and stir gently to mix with the sauce. Stir in the lime juice and sprinkle over the coriander, if using, and serve with rice and guacamole on the side.

Slow Cooker Mango Chicken

Servings: 4
Cooking Time: 4 Hours

Ingredients:

- 2 tbsp yellow curry paste
- 1 tsp ground turmeric
- 6 Coles RSPCA Approved Chicken Thigh Fillets, trimmed, halved crossways
- 500g pkt frozen mango cheeks, partially thawed, coarsely chopped (see note)
- 2 red capsicum, deseeded, thickly sliced
- 1 large red onion, cut into wedges
- 1 tbsp finely grated fresh ginger
- 3 garlic cloves, crushed
- 1 tbsp olive oil
- 200ml UHT coconut cream (see note)
- 1 tbsp brown sugar
- 2 green shallots, thinly sliced
- 2/3 cup fresh coriander leaves
- 1 fresh long red chilli, thinly sliced

- Lime wedges, to serve
- Steamed rice, to serve

Directions:

1. Combine the curry paste and turmeric in a large bowl. Add the chicken, season and toss well to combine. Set aside.
2. Place half the mango in a food processor and process until smooth. Transfer to the bowl of a slow cooker. Stir in 80ml (1/3 cup) water. Top with capsicum, onion, ginger and garlic.
3. Heat oil in a large frying pan over medium-high heat. Add chicken and cook, turning, for 5 minutes or until golden brown. Add to the slow cooker bowl. Cover and cook on Low for 3 hours or until the chicken is starting to become tender.
4. Add coconut cream to the slow cooker. Cover and cook on High for 1 hour or until the sauce thickens slightly. Stir in the remaining mango along with the sugar. Cook for a further 10 minutes or until the mango has warmed through. Turn off slow cooker and set aside for 5 minutes to rest.
5. Divide rice among serving plates. Add chicken and sprinkle with with green shallots, coriander and chilli. Serve with lime wedges.

NOTES

When mango is in season, substitute 500g of fresh mango pieces for this recipe.

UHT coconut cream has been heat-treated and although rich and creamy it doesn't curdle in the slow cooker. Swap for a 270ml can coconut cream if unavailable.

Pancetta And Mushroom-stuffed Chicken Breast

Servings: 4
Cooking Time: 30 Minutes

Ingredients:

- 4 slices pancetta
- 1 tablespoon olive oil
- 1 shallot, finely chopped
- 3/4 cup chopped fresh mushrooms
- 1/4 teaspoon salt, divided
- 1/4 teaspoon pepper, divided
- 4 boneless skinless chicken breast halves (6 ounces each)
- 1/2 cup prepared pesto

Directions:

1. Preheat oven to 350°. In a large skillet, cook pancetta over medium heat until partially cooked but not crisp; drain on paper towels.
2. In same skillet, heat oil over medium-high heat. Add shallot; cook and stir until lightly browned, 1-2 minutes. Stir in mushrooms; cook until tender, 1-2 minutes. Add 1/8 teaspoon salt and 1/8 teaspoon pepper.
3. Pound chicken breasts with a meat mallet to 1/4-in. thickness. Spread each with 2 tablespoons pesto; layer with 1 slice pancetta and a fourth of the mushroom mixture. Fold chicken in half, enclosing filling; secure with toothpicks. Sprinkle with remaining salt and pepper.
4. Transfer to a greased 13x9-in. baking dish. Bake until a thermometer inserted in chicken reads 165°, 30-35 minutes. Discard toothpicks before serving.

Italian-style Slow Cooker Chicken

Servings: 6
Cooking Time: 3 Hours 20 Minutes

Ingredients:

- 1 tbsp olive oil
- 4 Coles RSPCA Approved Australian Chicken Thigh Cutlets
- 4 Coles RSPCA Approved Australian Chicken Drumsticks
- 1 red onion, cut into wedges
- 1 red capsicum, seeded, coarsely chopped
- 1 yellow capsicum, seeded, coarsely chopped
- 2 garlic cloves, crushed
- 2 anchovy fillets, finely chopped
- 1 tbsp finely chopped oregano
- 1/2 cup (125ml) dry white wine
- 400g can cherry tomatoes

- 1 cup (250ml) chicken stock
- 1/2 cup (80g) Sicilian olives

Directions:
1. Heat the oil in a large frying pan or flameproof casserole pan over medium-high heat. Cook combined chicken, in 2 batches, turning occasionally, for 5 mins or until golden brown. Transfer to a plate.
2. Add onion and combined capsicum to pan. Cook, stirring, for 5 mins or until onion softens. Add the garlic, anchovy and oregano and cook, stirring, for 1 min or until aromatic. Return chicken to pan and pour over wine. Bring to the boil.
3. Transfer the chicken mixture to a slow cooker. Add the tomato, stock and olives. Cover and cook for 3 hours on high (or 6 hours on low) or until chicken is almost falling off the bone and sauce thickens slightly. Season.

NOTES
SERVE WITH - basil and oregano leaves

Slow Cooker Green Chile Cheesy Chicken

Servings: 6
Cooking Time: 4 Hours

Ingredients:
- 2 lbs. boneless skinless chicken thighs
- 1/2 tsp. salt
- 1/4 tsp. pepper
- 1 tsp. chili powder
- 1 1/2 cups green salsa I use Mrs. Renfros Jalapeno salsa, though a tomatillo salsa would work fine
- 1 poblano pepper diced
- 1 1/2 cups shredded Colby-Jack Cheese
- Rice for serving

Directions:
1. Add the chicken to the slow cooker.
2. Sprinkle over the salt, pepper and chili powder.
3. Sprinkle over the diced poblano chile and pour over the salsa.

4. Cover and cook on HIGH for 4 hours, or about 6 on low would work fine too.
5. When the cooking time is done, sprinkle over the cheese.
6. Cover the slow cooker for about 10 more minutes or until the cheese is melted.
7. Serve over rice if desired. Enjoy!

Chicken Cordon Bleu Sliders

Servings: 2
Cooking Time: 2 Hours

Ingredients:
- 1-1/2 pounds boneless skinless chicken breasts
- 1 garlic clove, minced
- 1/4 teaspoon salt
- 1/4 teaspoon pepper
- 1 package (8 ounces) cream cheese, cubed
- 2 cups shredded Swiss cheese
- 1-1/4 cups finely chopped fully cooked ham
- 2 packages (12 ounces each) Hawaiian sweet rolls, split
- Chopped green onions

Directions:
1. Place chicken in a greased 3-qt. slow cooker; sprinkle with garlic, salt and pepper. Top with cream cheese. Cook, covered, on low for 2-1/2 to 3 hours until a thermometer inserted in chicken reads 165°. Remove chicken; shred with 2 forks. Return to slow cooker.
2. Stir in Swiss cheese and ham. Cover and let stand 15 minutes or until cheese is melted. Stir before serving on rolls. Sprinkle with green onions.

Slow Cooker Thai Green Curry

Servings: 4
Cooking Time: 3 Hours

Ingredients:
- 800 g chicken thighs, skin on and bone in
- 1 tbsp. oil
- 4 tbsp. Thai green curry paste
- 2 tbsp. Nam Pla fish sauce

- 1 sweet potato, peeled and cut into 3cm (11/4in) pieces
- 1 aubergine, cut into 3cm (11/4in) pieces
- 150 g exotic mushrooms, sliced if large
- 1 red chilli, deseeded and sliced
- 400 ml tin coconut milk

Directions:

1. Heat oil in a large frying pan over medium/high heat and fry chicken, skin side down, for 10min, until skin is golden brown and crispy.
2. Transfer browned chicken to the bowl of a slow cooker, together with all remaining ingredients. Stir in 1tsp fine salt. Cover and cook on low for 2hr 50min, or until sweet potato is cooked. Serve with rice, if you like.
3. If you prefer a thicker curry, strain all of the liquid from the curry into a pan, setting aside the veg and chicken. In a small bowl, mix 11/2tbsp cornflour with 2tbsp of the curry liquid to make a paste. Add mixture to the pan and bring to a boil, stirring. Bubble for a few min, stirring occasionally, until thickened. Remove from the heat and return veg and chicken to the pan to reheat. Serve.

Slow-cooker Chicken Enchilada Dip

Servings: 8

Ingredients:

- 1 rotisserie chicken, shredded
- 1 15-oz. can enchilada sauce
- 2 c. pepper jack, grated
- 8 oz. cream cheese, softened
- 1 jalapeño, sliced
- 1 tbsp. Taco Seasoning
- Tortilla chips, for serving

Directions:

1. In a slow-cooker, combine chicken, enchilada sauce, pepper jack, cream cheese, jalapeño, and taco seasoning. Cover and cook on high, 1 hour.
2. Stir until creamy, then cook, covered, on low, 30 minutes to 1 hour.

3. Serve with tortilla chips.

Chicken-and-quinoa Minestrone

Servings: 4

Ingredients:

- For the Soup
- 1 onion, chopped
- 2 carrots, sliced
- 1 small fennel bulb, thinly sliced
- 2 garlic cloves, chopped
- 6 c. chicken stock
- 1 28-oz. can diced tomatoes
- 1 15-oz can kidney beans, rinsed
- 2 tsp. dried basil
- 2 tsp. dried oregano
- 1 bay leaf
- 1 Parmesan rind (optional)
- Kosher salt
- Freshly ground black pepper
- 4 bone-in chicken thighs, skin removed
- 2/3 c. quinoa, rinsed
- 1/2 bunch kale, thick stems discarded and leaves torn
- 6 oz. green beans, trimmed and halved
- For the Garlicky Herb Sauce
- 1 c. fresh flat-leaf parsley
- 1 c. fresh basil
- 1 garlic clove
- 1 tbsp. fresh lemon zest
- 1/3 c. extra-virgin olive oil
- 1/4 tsp. red pepper flakes
- Kosher salt
- Freshly ground black pepper

Directions:

1. Combine onion, carrots, fennel, garlic, stock, tomatoes, beans, basil, oregano, bay leaf, Parmesan rind (if desired), and 1/2 teaspoon each salt and pepper in a 6-quart slow cooker. Top with chicken. Cover and cook until vegetables are tender and

chicken is cooked through, on low for 7 to 8 hours or high for 4 to 5 hours.

2. Discard bay leaf and cheese rind. Remove chicken, discard bones, and shred meat; return to the slow cooker.

3. Stir in quinoa, kale, and green beans. Cover and cook until quinoa is tender, 30 to 40 minutes. Season with salt and pepper.

4. Make the Garlicky Herb Sauce: Pulse parsley, basil, garlic, lemon zest, olive oil, and red pepper flakes in a food processor until finely chopped, 15 to 20 times. Season with kosher salt and freshly ground black pepper.

Gingery Slow Cooker Chicken With Cabbage Slaw

Servings: 4

Ingredients:

- 1/4 c. apricot jam
- 2 tbsp. ketchup
- 1/4 c. soy sauce
- 2 tbsp. grated fresh ginger
- 2 lb. boneless, skinless chicken thighs, trimmed of excess fat
- 4 cloves garlic, chopped
- 1 medium onion, chopped
- 1 small red jalapeño pepper, chopped
- 1/4 c. unseasoned rice vinegar, divided
- Kosher salt and freshly ground black pepper
- 1 c. long-grain white rice
- 1/4 small red cabbage (about 8 ounces), cored and thinly sliced
- 2 scallions, sliced
- 1 tbsp. chopped fresh cilantro, plus more for serving
- 1 tbsp. olive oil
- Toasted sesame seeds, for serving

Directions:

1. Combine apricot jam, ketchup, soy sauce, and ginger in a 5- to 6-quart slow cooker. Add chicken, garlic, onion, and jalapeño; toss to coat. Cook,

covered, until chicken is cooked through, 3 1/2 to 4 1/2 hours on high or 5 1/2 to 6 1/2 hours on low. Transfer chicken to a plate and shred using two forks; return to slow cooker. Stir in 2 tablespoons rice vinegar. Season with salt and pepper.

2. Twenty-five minutes before serving, cook rice according to package directions. Toss together cabbage, scallions, cilantro, oil, and remaining 2 tablespoons rice vinegar in a bowl. Season with salt.

3. Serve chicken and sauce over rice topped with slaw, cilantro, and sesame seeds.

Freeze And Save One-pot Big-batch Chicken

Servings: 3
Cooking Time: 4 Hours 30 Minutes

Ingredients:

- 1 tbsp extra virgin olive oil
- 3kg chicken thigh fillets, fat trimmed
- 2 brown onions, finely chopped
- 5 garlic cloves, finely chopped
- 4 fresh bay leaves
- 250ml (1 cup) white wine
- 625ml (2 1/2 cups) Massel salt reduced chicken style liquid stock
- 2 large sprigs fresh continental parsley

Directions:

1. Heat the oil in a large non-stick frying pan over high heat. Season the chicken and cook, in 3-4 batches, for 10 minutes each batch or until golden. Transfer to the bowl of a 5-litre slow cooker.

2. Add the onion and garlic to the frying pan. Reduce the heat to medium and cook, stirring often, for 5 minutes or until golden. Add the bay leaves and wine and simmer for 5 minutes or until reduced. Add to the slow cooker.

3. Add the stock and parsley to the slow cooker. Cover and cook on low for 4 hours or until the chicken is tender. Cool. Divide among 3 shallow storage containers and freeze until required.

NOTES

Make this slow-cooker chicken ahead of time and freeze in batches.

Freezing tip:

When the chicken has stopped steaming, transfer to the three dishes, the more shallow the dish the faster it will cool. Seal and place in the fridge to cool completely and then transfer to the freezer.

Mediterranean Stuffed Chicken Breasts

Servings: 4
Cooking Time: 30 Minutes

Ingredients:

- 1 cup crumbled feta cheese
- 1/3 cup chopped oil-packed sun-dried tomatoes
- 4 boneless skinless chicken breast halves (6 ounces each)
- 2 tablespoons olive oil from sun-dried tomatoes, divided
- 1 teaspoon Greek seasoning

Directions:

1. Preheat oven to 375°. In a small bowl, mix cheese and tomatoes. Pound chicken breasts with a meat mallet to 1/4-in. thickness. Brush with 1 tablespoon oil; sprinkle with Greek seasoning. Top with cheese mixture. Roll up chicken from a short side; secure with a toothpick.

2. Place in a greased 11x7-in. baking dish, seam side down; brush with remaining oil. Bake, uncovered, 30-35 minutes or until until a thermometer reads 165°. Discard toothpicks before serving.

Slow Cooker Roast Chicken

Servings: 4
Cooking Time: 8 Hours

Ingredients:

- 1 whole chicken
- 250ml boiling water
- 2 chicken stock cubes
- 1/4 cup honey
- 1/4 cup lemon juice
- 1 tsp garlic crushed
- 1 onion chopped
- 1/2 lemon
- 3 tsp chicken gravy powder *to taste

Directions:

1. Add the chicken to the slow cooker.
2. Stuff the chicken with the onion and lemon.
3. Mix the stock cubes into the water.
4. Add honey, lemon juice and garlic to the stock, and then pour over the chicken.
5. Cook for 8 hours on low.

NOTES

Once cooked, remove chicken and add chicken Gravox to the liquid, whisk and you have a beautiful chicken gravy to complement the roast chicken.

MEAT RECIPES

Slow Cooker Beef Ragu With Pappardelle

Servings: 8

Ingredients:

- 1 teaspoon olive oil
- 6 garlic cloves, smashed slightly
- 1 1/2 pounds flank steak, cut against the grain into 4 pieces
- salt and pepper
- 1 (28 ounce) can crushed tomatoes
- 1/4 cup reduced sodium beef broth
- 1 carrot, chopped
- 2 bay leaves
- 2 sprigs fresh thyme
- 16 ounces pappardelle pasta
- Parmesan, ricotta, and parsley for topping

Directions:

1. In a small skillet, heat the oil over medium high heat. Add the garlic and cook, stirring, until golden and lightly browned, about 2 minutes.
2. Season the beef with 1 teaspoon salt and pepper to taste. Transfer to a 5- to 6-quart slow cooker. Pour the tomatoes and broth over the beef and add the garlic from step one, carrots, bay leaves, and thyme.
3. Cover and cook on high for 6 hours or on low for 8 to 10 hours. Discard the herbs and shred the beef in the pot using 2 forks.
4. Cook the pasta according to package directions. Drain, return to the pot, and add the sauce from the slow cooker. Increase the heat to high and cook, stirring, until the pasta and sauce are combined, about 1 minute.
5. Divide among 8 bowls and top each with Parmesan, ricotta, and parsley. Serve hot!

NOTES

Instant Pot Instructions: We followed the recipe as-is for 45 minutes on Manual and it turned out great. A quick release should work, but if it splatters, feel free to do a natural release.

Freeze Together:

6 cloves garlic, smashed

1 cup mirepoix, fresh or frozen

2 pounds flank steak or beef chuck, cut into 4 pieces

2 teaspoons salt

1 28-ounce can crushed tomatoes

1/2 teaspoon thyme

2 bay leaves

Instant Pot Instructions: High pressure 45 mins + 10 mins natural release

Slow Cooker Instructions: High setting 6 hours (thaw first)

Final Step: Shred the meat and serve with pasta, baked potatoes, polenta, rice, cauliflower rice, gnocchi, zucchini noodles, etc.

Beef Stew Cooked In White Wine Recipe

Servings: 4
Cooking Time: 2 Hours 40 Minutes

Ingredients:

- 75ml sunflower oil
- 425g fresh stewing beef, cut into large chunks
- 2 large carrots, peeled and chopped on the diagonal
- 2 onions, roughly chopped
- 1 clove garlic, minced
- 1tbsp tomato puree
- 1tbsp plain flour
- 350ml (12fl oz) white wine
- 500ml beef stock
- 1 bouquet garni
- 1 bay leaf
- salt
- pepper
- chive stalks, to garnish
- sprigs of parsley leaves, to garnish

Directions:

1. Pre-heat the oven to 150°C.
2. Heat most of the sunflower oil in a large, heavy-based casserole dish over a moderate heat until hot. Season the beef, then seal well on all sides until golden brown in colour. Remove from the pan then add the carrots, onion and garlic to the dish, stirring well and adding a little more sunflower oil if necessary.
3. Reduce the heat a little and let the vegetables soften, stirring occasionally, for 6-7 minutes. Add the tomato puree to the dish and the flour and stir well, allowing it to cook for a further minute or so. Add the beef back to the dish then cover with the white wine and beef stock. Bring to the boil, then add the bouquet garni.
4. Cover with a lid and transfer to the oven too cook gently for about 2 hours until the beef is tender and starting to break apart. Remove from the oven and discard the bouquet garni. Adjust the seasoning as necessary then spoon onto serving plates.
5. Garnish with chive stalks and a sprig of parsley leaves before serving.

4-ingredient Slow Cooker Lamb Shanks

Servings: 4
Cooking Time: 8 Hours

Ingredients:

- 4 lamb shanks
- 4 fresh rosemary sprigs, plus extra sprigs to serve
- 115g (⅓ cup) orange marmalade
- 40g packet French onion soup mix

Directions:

1. Place lamb shanks and rosemary in a slow cooker.
2. Whisk marmalade, soup mix and 1/2 cup water in a bowl until combined. Pour over lamb shanks. Cook, covered, on low for 8 hours or until lamb is tender. Alternatively, cook in a covered pot for 4 hours, but watch it closely so it doesn't burn.
3. Serve lamb shanks, with pan juices, sprinkled with extra rosemary.

NOTES
We used a tagine to make

Slow Cooker Satay Beef

Servings: 4
Cooking Time: 4 Hours

Ingredients:

- 1 tbs olive oil
- 1 1/4 kg beef chuck steak, cut into 3cm pieces
- 1 red capsicum deseeded cut into thick strips
- 250ml Ayam satay sauce
- 270ml coconut milk
- 1/2 cup coriander leaves *to serve
- 4 serves egg noodles cooked *to serve

Directions:

1. Heat the oil in a large frying pan over high heat. Add half of the beef. Cook, turning often for 6 minutes or until golden. Transfer to a slow cooker. Repeat with the remaining beef.
2. Add the satay sauce, coconut cream and capsicum to the slow cooker. Stir to combine. Cover and cook on high for 3 1/2 hours or until the beef is tender. Cook uncovered for 20 minutes. Serve scattered with coriander and egg noodles.

Slow Cooker Beef Brisket

Servings: 6-8
Cooking Time: 6 Hours 20 Minutes

Ingredients:

- 1 tbsp. vegetable oil
- 2 onions, thickly sliced
- 1 l gluten-free beef stock
- 4 garlic cloves, peeled
- 4 fresh bay leaves
- 2kg boned and rolled beef brisket
- For The Sauce
- 300 ml (10 fl oz (½ pint)) bourbon
- 100g light brown sugar
- 100g tomato ketchup
- 100 ml (3 ½ fl oz) cider vinegar
- 1/2 tbsp smoked paprika

- 1 tsp. cayenne pepper
- 2 tsp. ground cumin
- 1 tbsp. onion powder
- 1 tbsp. garlic granules

Directions:

1. In a large, deep frying pan, heat the oil and fry the onions over a high heat for 5min or until dark and golden, stirring occasionally. Stir in the stock, scraping the bottom of the pan and bring to the boil. Season well with pepper and a pinch of salt.
2. Put the brisket into the pan of the slow cooker (cut the brisket in half if you can't fit the whole piece in the pan), add the garlic cloves and bay leaves and pour over the hot cooking liquid. Cover with the lid and cook on low for 8hr, until the meat is tender and falling apart.
3. Meanwhile, make the sauce. Put all the ingredients except 1tbsp bourbon in a large pan and stir together over a medium heat, bubbling for 15-20min until thick. Stir in the remaining bourbon and season to taste. Set aside.
4. Lift the brisket out of the cooking liquid (see GH Tip) on to a board, and shred into pieces with two forks. Add the meat to the sauce in the pan and stir to coat. Serve.
5. GH Tip
6. You can use the cooking liquid as a base for another stew or soup.

Slow Cooker Beef Curry

Servings: 4-5
Cooking Time: 4 Hours 30 Minutes-8 Hours 30 Minutes

Ingredients:

- 750g beef for braising (braising steak, chuck, flank etc) cut into chunks
- 3 tbsp oil
- 1 onion, chopped
- 4 garlic cloves, crushed
- 5cm piece ginger, grated
- 4 cardamom pods
- 1 cinnamon stick

- 1 tbsp ground coriander
- 2 tsp ground cumin
- ½ tsp ground turmeric
- ½ – 1 tsp chilli powder
- 400ml coconut milk (see tip)
- small bunch coriander, chopped

Directions:

1. Heat your slow cooker if you need to. Fry the beef in batches in 2 tbsp oil until it is browned all over and tip into the slow cooker. Put the remaining oil in the frying pan and fry the onion over a low heat until it starts to soften. Add the garlic and ginger and fry for 1 minute.
2. Add all the spices and fry for 1 minute or until the spices start to smell fragrant. Add the coconut milk and bring to a simmer, then tip everything into the slow cooker.
3. Cook for 4 hours on high or 8 hours on low. Stir in the coriander and serve.
4. RECIPE TIPS
5. SWAP THE BASE
6. You can make this recipe tomato based if you like – add 400ml passata or a whizzed-up tin of tomatoes instead of the coconut milk.

Slow Cooker Shepherd's Pie

Servings: 6
Cooking Time: 6 Hours 25 Minutes

Ingredients:

- 1 tsp. vegetable oil
- 1 onion, finely chopped
- 300 g lamb mince, 10% fat or less
- 2 garlic cloves, crushed
- 1 tbsp. tomato purée
- Small handful thyme, leaves picked and roughly chopped
- 400 g tin green lentils, drained and rinsed
- 2 carrots, peeled and thinly sliced
- 500 g passata
- 1 beef stock cube, crumbled
- FOR THE MASH
- 600 g sweet potatoes, peeled and roughly chopped

- 200 g floury potatoes, peeled and roughly chopped, we used Maris Piper
- 25 g reduced fat butter, we used Lurpak Lighter
- 1/2 1tsp hot smoked paprika, to taste
- 40 g half fat crème fraîche

Directions:

1. Make the mash. Put all the potatoes in a large pan, cover with cold water and bring to the boil over high heat. Simmer for 15min, or until very tender.

2. Drain potatoes and leave to steam dry and cool slightly in a colander for 5min. Return potatoes to pan and mash until smooth with a potato masher. Add butter, paprika and crème fraîche, season well and stir together.

3. Meanwhile, heat the oil in a frying pan over medium heat. Add onion and fry for 10min, until softened. Add garlic and fry for 1min, until fragrant. Add the lamb, increase heat to high and fry until browned well all over. Stir in the tomato purée and thyme, cook for 2min.

4. Scrape lamb mixture into the bowl of a slow cooker and stir in the lentils, carrots, passata and crumbled stock cube. Spoon mash on top. Cover and cook on low for 6hr (see GH tip). Serve.

5. GH tip:

6. If the bowl of your slow cooker is oven-safe (check the manual first, to be certain), transfer to a hot grill for a few min to brown the top before serving, if you like.

Slow-cooked Mexican Pork Pibil

Servings: 6-8
Cooking Time: 3 Hours 35 Minutes

Ingredients:

- 1 tbsp. allspice berries
- 2 tsp. cumin seeds
- 1 tsp. black peppercorns
- 1 onion, roughly chopped
- 4 garlic cloves
- 1 scotch bonnet chilli, deseeded and roughly chopped

- 50 g (2oz) annatto paste, we used El Yucateco
- 100 ml (3 ½ fl oz) white wine vinegar
- Juice 4 oranges
- 1 (3 ½lb) boneless pork shoulder
- 2 bay leaves
- Corn tortillas, soured cream, avocado and coriander, to serve
- FOR THE PICKLED RED ONIONS (OPTIONAL)
- 175 ml (6 fl oz) white wine vinegar
- 3 tbsp. caster sugar
- 1 tsp. allspice berries
- 1/2 tsp salt
- 1 bay leaf
- 2 red onions, thinly sliced

Directions:

1. Heat a medium frying pan and dry fry the allspice berries, cumin seeds and peppercorns for a few minutes until fragrant. Transfer to a pestle and mortar and grind to a fine powder.

2. Put the spice powder in a food processor or blender with the onion, garlic, chilli and annatto paste and blend until finely chopped. Add the white wine vinegar and the orange juice and blend until combined.

3. Trim pork of skin and excess fat (leaving a thin layer). Cut the joint into four large pieces. Put into a non-metallic bowl and pour over the marinade. Stir in the bay leaves. Cover, refrigerate and marinate for at least an hour, or ideally overnight.

4. Preheat oven to 160°C (140°C fan) mark 3. Transfer pork and marinade to a large casserole. Heat on the hob, until simmering. Cover the casserole with a lid and transfer to the oven; cook for 2½hr, basting the pork every now and again.

5. Remove the lid, increase the temperature to 170°C (150°C fan) mark 3 and continue to cook for 1hr until the pork is tender and the sauce has thickened.

6. Meanwhile, make the pickled onions. Put all the ingredients apart from the onions into a small pan; heat until the sugar dissolves. Remove from heat and mix in the onions. Leave for at least 1hr, stirring occasionally, until the onions have softened.

7. Remove bay leaves from the pork. Using 2 forks, shred pork in the sauce and serve with tortillas, soured cream, avocado, coriander and pickled onions.

8. GET AHEAD Up to 2 days ahead, cook and shred pork, allow to cool, then store with the sauce, covered, in the fridge. To reheat: transfer to a pan, bring up to simmer, adding a splash of water if needed, then cover and simmer until piping hot. Pickle the onions up to 5 days ahead and store in a non-metallic bowl.

9. GH TIP We used Mexican corn tortillas to make this gluten free, but you could use flour ones, if you like.

Slow Cooker Corned Beef In Ginger Beer

Servings: 6
Cooking Time: 10 Hours

Ingredients:
- 1 1/2 kg corned beef
- 1 onion large
- 4 whole cloves
- 1 1/4 L ginger beer

Directions:
1. Peel onion, but leave whole. Stud with the fresh cloves.
2. Place onion and corned beef into slow cooker. Pour over ginger beer until meat is covered.
3. Cook on low for 8-10 hours.
4. If meat is not required straight away, wrap in aluminium foil and refrigerate.

NOTES
Corned beef responds very well to long slow cooking, I usually cook mine overnight. The meat will have a very slight flavour of ginger, but the flavour works in beautifully with the meat. Excellent the next day on sandwiches, and with salads.

Slow Cooker Beef Ragu

Servings: 8
Cooking Time: 8 Hours

Ingredients:
- 3-4 pound boneless beef roast
- salt and black pepper
- 2 tablespoons olive oil
- 1 small yellow onion diced
- 4 cloves of garlic finely minced
- 2 28- ounce cans San Marzano Tomatoes one can drained
- 3 tablespoons tomato paste
- 3/4 cup red wine
- 1 teaspoon dried oregano
- 1 teaspoon dried basil
- 1/2 teaspoon dried thyme
- 1/2 teaspoon dried parsley
- 1/2 teaspoon crushed red pepper
- dry pasta of choice cooked per manufacturer's Directions:
- fresh parsley for garnish
- grated parmesan cheese for serving

Directions:
1. Season the beef with salt and black pepper. In a large non-stick deep skillet, heat the olive oil over medium high heat. Add the beef roast and brown on all sides, about 10 minutes. Remove from heat.
2. Transfer the beef roast to the slow cooker. Also to the slow cooker, add the onion, garlic, tomatoes (add the liquid from one can only), tomato paste, red wine, oregano, basil, thyme, parsley, crushed red pepper and a generous amount of salt and black pepper. Slow cook on low for 6-8 hours or until the beef is falling apart.
3. Shred the beef with two forks and mix well. Serve the beef ragu over pasta, garnished with fresh parsley and grated parmesan cheese. Enjoy!

Slow Cooker Bone Broth

Servings: 4
Cooking Time: 36 Hours

Ingredients:

- Beef, veal bones and or chicken, ask your butcher what they have
- 2 carrots, roughly chopped
- 1 leek, roughly chopped
- 1 celery stick, roughly chopped
- juice 1 lemon
- 1 bay leaf

Directions:

1. Heat oven to 180C/160C fan/gas 4. Spread the bones out on a baking sheet and roast them for an hour, turning them over after 30 mins.
2. Heat the slow cooker if necessary. Pack the veg into the slow cooker, add the bones and enough water to fill the pot to within 2cm of the top. Add the lemon juice and the bay leaves. Cover and cook on Low for 18-36 hours. The longer you cook the broth the darker it will become.
3. Place a colander over a bowl and scoop out all the bones into the colander. Return any broth from the bowl to the pan. Strain all the liquid through a fine sieve. Taste, and season only if you need to. Allow the broth to cool and lift off the fat. Store in the fridge for up to 3 days or transfer to freezer bags once it has cooled.

Slow-cooker Meatballs With Fettuccine

Servings: 6
Cooking Time: 4 Hours 25 Minutes

Ingredients:

- 500g Coles Australian No Added Hormones Beef 3 Star Mince
- 2 Coles Australian Classic Pork Sausages, casings removed
- 1 brown onion, coarsely grated
- 1 cup (70g) fresh breadcrumbs (made from day-old bread)
- 1 Coles Australian Free Range Egg, lightly whisked
- 2 tsp finely chopped sage
- 2 tsp finely chopped oregano
- 2 tsp finely chopped basil
- 1 tbsp olive oil
- 1 brown onion, extra, finely chopped
- 2 garlic cloves, crushed
- 1/2 cup (125ml) dry red wine or beef stock
- 400g can diced tomatoes
- 400g jar tomato pasta sauce
- 500g fettuccine

Directions:

1. Place beef mince, sausage mince, grated onion, breadcrumbs, egg, sage, oregano and basil in a large bowl. Use your hands to mix until well combined. Season. Shape tablespoonfuls of mince mixture into balls. Place on a plate.
2. Heat the oil in a frying pan over medium heat. Add the meatballs. Cook, turning, for 5 mins or until brown all over. Transfer to a slow cooker.
3. Add the chopped onion to the pan. Cook, stirring, for 5 mins or until onion softens. Add garlic and cook for 1 min or until aromatic. Add the wine or beef stock and bring to the boil. Add the tomato and pasta sauce and stir to combine. Pour over the meatballs in the slow cooker. Cover. Cook for 4 hours on high (or 6 hours on low) or until the meatballs are cooked through and sauce thickens slightly. Season. (To freeze now, see tip below.)
4. Cook the pasta in a large saucepan of boiling water following packet directions or until al dente. Drain well. Return the pasta to the pan with a little of the sauce from the slow cooker. Toss to combine. Divide the pasta mixture evenly among serving bowls. Spoon over the meatballs and sauce.

NOTES
SERVE WITH shaved parmesan and basil leaves

Slow-cooker Brisket

Servings: 6-8

Ingredients:

- 3 lb. beef brisket
- 1 small white onion, sliced
- 2 garlic cloves, smashed and peeled
- 2 c. low sodium chicken stock
- 2 sprigs fresh thyme
- Kosher salt
- Freshly ground black pepper

Directions:

1. Place all ingredients in slow cooker and season with salt and pepper. Cover and cook 6 to 8 hours on low, or until brisket is completely tender.
2. Remove from slow cooker to slice. Serve with jus.

Provençal Daube Of Beef Recipe

Servings: 4
Cooking Time: 2 Hours 40 Minutes

Ingredients:

- 1 tbsp olive oil
- 625g rolled brisket
- 2 red onions, sliced
- 1 garlic clove, crushed
- 400ml beef stock
- 200ml white wine
- bouquet garni
- pinch ground cloves
- ½ orange, zested
- 4 carrots
- 8 small potatoes
- 4 celery sticks

Directions:

1. Heat the oven to gas 3, 160°C, fan 140°C. On the hob heat the oil in an ovenproof dish, add the beef and brown well all over on the outside.
2. Remove the beef, then add the onions and garlic and cook gently for 5 mins, pour in the stock and wine (use extra stock instead of wine if preferred) and mix well. Add the bouquet garni, ground cloves and orange zest, and return the beef to the pan. Cover with a lid and cook in the oven for 2 hrs.
3. Add the carrots (peeled and chopped into quarters) and potatoes (cleaned but unpeeled) to the casserole, replace the lid and cook for a further 20 mins. Then add the celery sticks (cut in half) and cook for another 10 mins.
4. Remove the beef from the pan and carve. Serve with the veggies and juices and season with salt and pepper.
5. Freezing
6. In order to enjoy optimum flavour and quality, frozen items are best used within 3 months of their freezing date.

Slow-cooked Pork & Red Cabbage

Servings: 2
Cooking Time: 2 Hours-2 Hours 15 Minutes

Ingredients:

- 1.5kg/3lb 5oz pork shoulder
- 1 rounded tsp black peppercorns
- 1 tbsp thyme leaves
- 3 tbsp olive oil
- 2 onions, chopped
- 1.5kg red cabbage, finely shredded
- 2 apples, peeled, cored and cut into eighths
- 425ml red wine
- 200g pack vacuum-packed chestnuts
- 2 tbsp cranberry or redcurrant jelly

Directions:

1. Heat oven to 160C/fan 140C/gas 3. Cut the pork into thick slices, about 3cm thick. Coarsely crush the peppercorns and sprinkle over the pork along with the thyme and some salt and pepper.
2. Heat 2 tbsp oil in a large flameproof casserole, then add the onions and fry until lightly browned. Add the cabbage and stir well, then add the apples and wine and cook until the cabbage starts to soften. Finally, add the chestnuts, 1 tbsp of the jelly, salt and pepper, and bring to the boil. Cover and simmer for 5 mins.

3. Meanwhile, heat 1 tbsp of the oil in a frying pan, add the pork and fry on both sides until browned, then stir in the remaining tbsp of the jelly. Cook for a few mins until the pork is deeply browned and glistening. Arrange the pork over the cabbage. Pour a little boiling water into the frying pan, stir well to lift up all the pan juices, then pour over the pork.

4. Cover the pan tightly, then cook in the oven for 1¼-1½ hrs until the pork is very tender.

5. RECIPE TIPS

6. FREEZING

7. Freeze at the end of step 4. Defrost in the fridge overnight. Add a little more water if it looks dry, then bring to the boil. Return to the oven at 160C/fan 140C/gas 3 for 20-25 mins until heated through.

Chilli Con Carne Recipe

Servings: 4
Cooking Time: 1 Hours

Ingredients:

- 1 large onion
- 1 red pepper
- 2 garlic cloves
- 1 tbsp oil
- 1 heaped tsp hot chilli powder (or 1 level tbsp if you only have mild)
- 1 tsp paprika
- 1 tsp ground cumin
- 500g lean minced beef
- 1 beef stock cube
- 400g can chopped tomatoes
- ½ tsp dried marjoram
- 1 tsp sugar
- 2 tbsp tomato purée
- 410g can red kidney beans
- plain boiled long grain rice, to serve
- soured cream, to serve

Directions:

1. Prepare your vegetables. Chop 1 large onion into small dice, about 5mm square. The easiest way to do this is to cut the onion in half from root to tip, peel it and slice each half into thick matchsticks lengthways, not quite cutting all the way to the root end so they are still held together. Slice across the matchsticks into neat dice.

2. Cut 1 red pepper in half lengthways, remove stalk and wash the seeds away, then chop. Peel and finely chop 2 garlic cloves.

3. Start cooking. Put your pan on the hob over a medium heat. Add 1 tbsp oil and leave it for 1-2 minutes until hot (a little longer for an electric hob).

4. Add the onion and cook, stirring fairly frequently, for about 5 minutes, or until the onion is soft, squidgy and slightly translucent.

5. Tip in the garlic, red pepper, 1 heaped tsp hot chilli powder or 1 level tbsp mild chilli powder, 1 tsp paprika and 1 tsp ground cumin.

6. Give it a good stir, then leave it to cook for another 5 minutes, stirring occasionally.

7. Brown 500g lean minced beef. Turn the heat up a bit, add the meat to the pan and break it up with your spoon or spatula. The mix should sizzle a bit when you add the mince.

8. Keep stirring and prodding for at least 5 minutes, until all the mince is in uniform, mince-sized lumps and there are no more pink bits. Make sure you keep the heat hot enough for the meat to fry and become brown, rather than just stew.

9. Make the sauce. Crumble 1 beef stock cube into 300ml hot water. Pour this into the pan with the mince mixture.

10. Add a 400g can of chopped tomatoes. Tip in ½ tsp dried marjoram, 1 tsp sugar and add a good shake of salt and pepper. Squirt in about 2 tbsp tomato purée and stir the sauce well.

11. Simmer it gently. Bring the whole thing to the boil, give it a good stir and put a lid on the pan. Turn down the heat until it is gently bubbling and leave it for 20 minutes.

12. Check on the pan occasionally to stir it and make sure the sauce doesn't catch on the bottom of the pan or isn't drying out. If it is, add a couple of tablespoons of water and make sure that the heat really is low enough. After simmering gently, the saucy mince mixture should look thick, moist and juicy.

13. Drain and rinse a 410g can of red kidney beans in a sieve and stir them into the chilli pot. Bring to the boil again, and gently bubble without the lid for another 10 minutes, adding a little more water if it looks too dry.

14. Taste a bit of the chilli and season. It will probably take a lot more seasoning than you think.

15. Now replace the lid, turn off the heat and leave your chilli to stand for 10 minutes before serving. This is really important as it allows the flavours to mingle.

16. Serve with soured cream and plain boiled long grain rice.

17. RECIPE TIPS

18. A MEXICAN TWIST

19. Rather than add the teaspoon of sugar, you can stir in a small piece of chocolate (about the size of your thumbnail) when you add the beans. Any plain dark chocolate will do. Be careful not to add too much – you don't want to be able to identify the flavour of the chocolate.

20. OTHER WAYS TO ENJOY CHILLI

21. Serve it on a bed of plain, boiled rice, with a spoonful of soured cream on top. Pile it on tortilla chips and sprinkle it with grated cheddar. Wrap it up in a tortilla with shredded lettuce, chopped tomatoes and guacamole for a great burrito.

22. NEXT LEVEL CHILLI CON CARNE RECIPE

23. If you loved this, now try making our next level chilli con carne recipe for an extra special take on this classic.

Hearty Beef Pot-au-feu

Servings: 6
Cooking Time: 4 Hours

Ingredients:
- 800g Coles No Added Hormone Beef Brisket
- 500g beef cheek
- 6 baby onions
- 1 leek, well washed, cut into 4cm pieces
- 1 bunch baby carrots, trimmed
- 650g baby chat potatoes
- 2 stalks celery, cut into 3cm pieces
- 1 garlic clove, peeled
- 2 sprigs thyme
- 1 bay leaf
- 1 tsp black peppercorns
- 1L Massel beef stock
- 2 tbsp micro herbs, to serve
- Dijon mustard, crusty bread, to serve

Directions:
1. Place meat in a 5.5L (22 cup) slow cooker. Add vegetables, herbs, peppercorns and Massel Liquid Stock Beef Style. Cook, covered, on low for 8 hours or until beef is very tender.

2. Discard thyme and bay leaf.

3. Serve beef, vegetables and a little stock in shallow plates. Sprinkle with microherbs and serve with mustard and bread.

NOTES
Peel baby onions but leave roots so they hold together.

Slow Cooker Pork Vindaloo

Servings: 6
Cooking Time: 6 Minutes

Ingredients:
- 1kg round beef steak
- 1/4 cup plain flour
- 1 tbsp olive oil
- 2 brown onions, sliced
- 200g cup mushrooms, sliced
- 2 cloves garlic, crushed
- 2 large carrots, peeled and roughly chopped
- 400g tin crushed tomatoes
- 1 cup chicken or beef stock

Directions:
1. Cut steak into 6-8cm pieces and use a meat mallet to pound until 5mm thick. Season well with salt and pepper, then dust lightly in flour. Heat 2 tbsp oil in a frypan and brown beef on both sides. Transfer to a plate.

2. Heat remaining oil in frypan and cook onions for 4-5 minutes until soft. Add mushrooms and cook, stirring, until starting to soften. Add garlic and cook

for a further minute. Transfer mixture to the bowl of a slow cooker. Add carrots and seared beef. Pour in tomatoes and chicken stock. Cover with the lid and cook for 4 hours on high or 6 hours on low until beef is very tender and sauce has thickened and reduced.

3. Alternatively, cook in a covered casserole dish in the oven for 2 hours at 160C conventional.

NOTES

You can use any slow-cooking cut of beef - oyster blade, blade, chuck or round. Make sure to tenderise with a meat mallet.

You can skip all of the browning and pan-frying at the start and just toss it all in the slow cooker, but the end result is better if you take some time to start things well.

Slow Cooked Cola Pulled Pork Burgers

Servings: 6
Cooking Time: 8 Hours 15 Minutes

Ingredients:

- 1.2kg boneless pork shoulder, rind and fat removed
- 375ml can cola
- 3/4 cup barbecue sauce
- 1/2 tsp chilli powder (optional)
- 6 Coles Brioche Hamburger Buns, split, toasted
- 1/2 cup whole-egg mayonnaise
- 300g packet fine-cut coleslaw kit
- 1 cup fresh at-leaf parsley leaves
- 3 dill pickles, sliced
- Sweet potato chips, to serve

Directions:

1. Place pork in slow cooker. Combine cola, barbecue sauce and chilli powder, if using, in small bowl. Pour over the pork. Cover. Cook on LOW for 8 hours (or HIGH for 4 hours) or until pork is very tender.

2. Transfer pork to a heatproof dish. Using two forks, shred meat. Cover to keep warm. Strain pan juices into a small saucepan. Bring to the boil over medium-high heat. Boil for 15 minutes or until

thickened. Add sauce mixture to pork. Toss to combine.

3. Top bun bases with mayonnaise, pork mixture, coleslaw, parsley and pickles. Sandwich with bun tops. Serve with sweet potato chips.

NOTES

YOU'LL NEED A 5-LITRE SLOW COOKER FOR THIS RECIPE.

Slow Cooker Cabbage Rolls

Servings: 6

Ingredients:

- 1 lb. ground beef plus a touch of salt and pepper to season
- 3 lbs. peeled russet potatoes sliced a ¼ inch thick (about 7 cups total after being sliced)
- 1 cup thinly sliced white onion
- 1 tsp. paprika
- ½ tsp. garlic powder
- 1 tsp. parsley
- 1 tsp salt
- ¼ tsp. pepper
- 3 cups shredded sharp cheese
- ½ cup beef broth or chicken broth

Directions:

1. Brown the ground beef on the stove top, drain fat. Add a touch of salt and pepper to season.

2. In a small bowl combine the paprika, garlic powder, parsley, salt and pepper.

3. Add half of the potatoes in the slow cooker. Sprinkle over half of the onions, half of the seasonings, half of the meat, and half of the cheese. Repeat the layers again.

4. Drizzle over the broth evenly over the layers.

5. Cover and cook on high for 4 hours. Do not open the lid during the cooking time or the potatoes will not get soft.

NOTES

Can I use a different kind of potato?

Use any type of potatoes (red potatoes, gold potatoes, or white potatoes). Just be sure to thinly slice them.

You can even use sweet potatoes for an entirely different meal.

Can I use bacon instead of ground beef?

Yes, you can use 12-16 ounces of cooked and crumbled bacon instead of ground beef.

Slow-cooker Spicy Pineapple Roast Pork With Lemongrass And Lime Rice

Servings: 8
Cooking Time: 8 Hours 40 Minutes

Ingredients:

- 2kg boneless pork leg
- 1 1/2 cups pineapple juice
- 1/4 cup soy sauce
- 2 garlic cloves, peeled, halved
- 2 tbsp lime juice, plus lime halves to serve
- 2 tbsp fish sauce
- 2 lemongrass stalks, trimmed, halved
- 2 long red chillies, thickly sliced, plus extra thinly sliced to serve
- 1 tsp sea salt
- 1 Lebanese cucumber, sliced diagonally
- 1 carrot, cut into long matchsticks
- 1/2 cup fresh coriander sprigs
- Lemongrass and lime rice
- 2 cups jasmine rice, rinsed
- 1/3 cup lime juice
- 2 lemongrass stalks, trimmed, halved
- 2 tsp lime zest

Directions:

1. Remove and discard string from pork. Using a sharp knife, carefully remove rind from pork. Place rind on a plate. Refrigerate.
2. Place pork in slow cooker. Add pineapple juice, soy sauce, garlic, lime juice, fish sauce, lemongrass and chilli. Cover. Cook on LOW for 8 hours (or HIGH for 4 hours), turning pork halfway through cooking, or until very tender. Turn slow cooker off.
3. Preheat oven to 220C/200C fan-forced. Cut 1/2 of the reserved rind into 2cm-thick strips. Discard

remaining rind. Sprinkle with sea salt. Set aside for 10 minutes. Place rind on a rack set over a baking tray. Roast for 30 to 35 minutes or until golden and puffed.

4. Meanwhile, make lemongrass and lime rice. Place rice, 3 cups water, lime juice and lemongrass in a large saucepan over high heat. Bring to the boil. Reduce heat to low. Cover. Simmer gently for 12 minutes or until liquid is absorbed and rice is tender. Remove from heat. Stand for 5 minutes. Fluff rice with a fork. Stir in the lime zest. Season with salt and pepper.
5. Remove pork from cooking liquid. Using two forks, roughly shred meat. Arrange pork, rice, cucumber and carrot in serving bowls. Drizzle with cooking liquid. Top with extra chilli, pork crackling and coriander. Serve with lime halves.

NOTES

To make in the pressure cooker: Follow steps 1 and 2, placing ingredients in a pressure cooker. Seal cooker. Place over high heat until steam escapes at a constant rate. Reduce heat to low. Cook for 1 hour 40 minutes. Release steam following manufacturer's instructions. Continue from

Slow Cooker Pork Ragu

Servings: 4

Ingredients:

- 1 can whole tomatoes
- 4 clove garlic
- 2 medium carrots
- 1 large onion
- 1/2 c. dry white wine
- 2 tsp. dried oregano
- Kosher salt and pepper
- 2 1/2 lb. pork shoulder
- 12 oz. pappardelle or other wide noodle
- 1/2 c. fresh flat-leaf parsley
- 1/4 c. grated Parmesan (1 oz)

Directions:

1. In a 5- to 6-qt slow cooker, combine the tomatoes, garlic, carrots, onion, wine, oregano, and 1/2 tsp each salt and pepper.
2. Add the pork to the slow cooker and cook, covered, until the pork is cooked through and easily pulls apart, 6 to 8 hours on low or 4 to 5 hours on high.
3. Twenty minutes before serving, cook the pasta according to package directions. Using a fork, break the meat into smaller pieces, then stir it into its cooking liquid; fold in the parsley. Serve the pork over the pasta and sprinkle with the Parmesan.
4. Tips
5. Freeze the ragu for up to 3 months. Thaw in the refrigerator overnight. Reheat in a large saucepan, covered, over medium heat, about 10 minutes (if it starts to dry out, add 1/4 to 1/2 cup water or chicken broth).

Braised Lamb Shanks With Potatoes, Olives And Lemon

Cooking Time: 3 Hours 15 Minutes

Ingredients:

- 4 French-trimmed lamb shanks
- 1/4 cup (35g) plain flour
- 1/3 cup (80ml) extra virgin olive oil
- 3 garlic cloves, bruised
- 1 red onion, thinly sliced
- 1 carrot, roughly chopped
- 1 celery stalk, roughly chopped
- 3 thyme sprigs, plus extra thyme leaves to serve
- 3/4 cup (185ml) white wine
- 2 cups (500ml) chicken or beef stock
- 3 desiree potatoes (about 600g), peeled, cut into wedges
- 3/4 cup (150g) pitted mixed olives
- Finely grated zest of 1 lemon

Directions:

1. Dust the lamb in flour. Heat 2 tbs oil in a large casserole over medium-high heat. Season the lamb, then cook, turning, for 6-8 minutes until browned. Remove from pan and set aside.

2. Reduce heat to medium and add the garlic, onion, carrot, celery, thyme and remaining 2 tbs oil. Cook for 2-3 minutes until fragrant. Return lamb to the casserole and season. Increase heat to high and add wine, scraping the bottom of pan. Cook for 1-2 minutes until evaporated. Add stock and enough water to cover lamb. Reduce heat to low, then cover with a lid and cook for 2 hours.
3. Add potatoes and olives, cover and cook for a further 45 minutes or until the lamb is very tender and potatoes are cooked through. Remove the lid and simmer for 10-15 minutes until reduced by one-third. Remove from heat and season.
4. Sprinkle lamb shanks with lemon zest and extra thyme leaves to serve.

Slow Cooker Asian Pork Roast Recipe

Servings: 6
Cooking Time: 4 Hours-8 Hours

Ingredients:

- 900g pork leg steaks
- 1tbsp vegetable oil
- 1inch/3cm piece ginger peeled and finely chopped
- 3 garlic cloves sliced
- 2 long red chillies, seeded and sliced
- 3 whole star anise
- 1tbsp honey
- 150ml hoisin sauce
- 250ml/1 cup of sherry

Directions:

1. Turn the slow cooker on. Heat a large frying pan with the oil. Season the meat well and then brown on all sides. Remove from the pan and then sauté the ginger, garlic and one of the chilis for 5 minutes. Pour in the hoisin, rice wine or sherry and star anise. Stir to mix well.
2. Place the roast in the slow cooker. Pour the sauce over and place the lid on. Cook on low heat for 8 hours or high heat for 4 hours. Do not lift the lid while cooking as it will take longer.

3. Serve over rice with the remaining red chili and some chopped spring onions.
4. Freezing and defrosting guidelines
5. Cook as instructed and allow to cool completely. Then transfer to an airtight, freezer-safe container, seal and freeze for up to 1-3 months. To serve, defrost thoroughly in the fridge overnight before reheating. To reheat and serve, place on medium heat, stirring occasionally until the dish is heated through.

Slow-cooker Korean Beef

Servings: 6

Ingredients:
- 1 small rump roast (3 to 4 lbs.)
- 3 c. beef broth
- 1 c. low-sodium soy sauce
- 1/2 c. brown sugar
- 4 cloves Garlic, Chopped
- 3 tbsp. sesame oil
- Juice of 3 limes
- 2 tbsp. sriracha
- Cooked jasmine rice, for serving
- Green onions, for serving

Directions:
1. In a 6-quart slow-cooker, combine rump roast, beef broth, soy sauce, brown sugar, garlic, sesame oil, lime juice, and Sriracha. Cover and cook on low, 8 hours.
2. When ready to eat, transfer beef to a cutting board and shred. Pour over enough broth until nicely saucy, then serve over rice with green onions.

Slow-cooker Ham With Sticky Ginger Glaze

Servings: 6-8
Cooking Time: 7 Hours 20 Minutes

Ingredients:
- 1 onion, thickly sliced
- 10 cloves, plus extra for studding
- 1 medium gammon joint, approx 1.3kg
- 1.5 litre bottle ginger beer
- 1 tbsp English mustard
- 3 tbsp ginger preserve

Directions:
1. Put the onion and 10 cloves in the base of the slow cooker then nestle in the gammon joint. Pour over the ginger beer then cover and cook on LOW for 7 hours until the gammon is tender, but still holding its shape. You can cool then chill the gammon at this stage if you prefer.
2. Heat the oven to 200C/180C fan/ gas 6. Carefully remove the skin from the gammon leaving a layer of fat behind. Score the fat in a diamond pattern with a sharp knife, making sure you don't cut into the meat, then stud the centre of each diamond with cloves.
3. Mix the mustard and ginger preserve in a bowl, spoon or brush over the gammon then bake for 20 mins until golden and sticky. If roasting from cold you will need to add another 20 mins to the cooking time.

FISH AND SEAFOOD RECIPES

Slow Cooker Barbacoa

Servings: 4
Cooking Time: 7 Hours

Ingredients:

- 4 tomatoes, quartered
- 2 dried ancho chillies, seeds removed
- 1 tsp dried oregano
- 1 tsp cumin seeds
- 1 garlic bulb, cloves peeled
- 400ml red wine
- ½ lamb shoulder, bone in (about 1.25kg)
- 50g dark chocolate, broken into squares
- 1 cinnamon stick
- 8 large new potatoes, about 450g
- white cabbage & radish slaw , to serve

Directions:

1. Put the tomatoes, chillies, oregano, cumin and garlic in a food processor with one-third of the wine, add 1 tsp salt and blitz until smooth.
2. Put the lamb in the slow cooker pot (we used a 6.5-litre model). Pour over the chilli mix, then add the rest of the wine with the chocolate, cinnamon stick and whole potatoes. Cover and cook on low for 7 hrs until the lamb is really tender and the potatoes are still firm.
3. To serve, remove the bones and skin from the lamb and pull the meat apart into large chunks. Chop the potatoes into chunks and skim the fat from the cooking juices. Serve the lamb, potato and juices in bowls with the slaw on top.
4. RECIPE TIPS
5. CHILLI SEEDS
6. If you have trouble getting the seeds out of the dried chillies, pour boiling water over them and leave for just 1-2 mins – they will quickly soften enough to cut them open.

Slow Cooker Scalloped Potatoes

Servings: 10-12

Ingredients:

- 5 tbsp. unsalted butter, divided
- 1 small yellow onion, chopped
- 3 garlic cloves, chopped
- 1 1/2 tbsp. all-purpose flour
- 2 1/2 c. heavy cream
- 4 tsp. kosher salt
- 2 tsp. chopped fresh thyme, plus more for garnish
- 1 1/2 tsp. black pepper, plus more for garnish
- 1 1/2 c. sharp white Cheddar cheese, shredded
- 1 1/2 c. Gruyere cheese, shredded
- 4 lb. Russet potatoes (about 4 large potatoes), peeled
- Nonstick cooking spray

Directions:

1. 1In a large skillet, heat 2 tablespoons of the butter over medium heat. Add the onion and cook, stirring occasionally, until softened, 4 to 6 minutes. Add the garlic and cook, stirring occasionally, until fragrant, about 1 minute.
2. 2Add the remaining 3 tablespoons of the butter to the skillet over medium low heat. Add the flour and cook, stirring constantly, until smooth and very lightly browned, about 1 minute. Gradually whisk in the cream until smooth and well combined. Whisk in the salt, thyme, and pepper. Bring the mixture to a simmer, whisking constantly, over medium heat. Remove from heat and whisk in the Cheddar and Gruyere.
3. 3Using a mandoline or slicer, slice the potatoes into 1/8-inch slices (very thin).
4. 4Lightly grease a 6-quart slow cooker with nonstick cooking spray. Layer about 1/3 of the potato slices in the slow cooker and top with 1/3 of the cheese mixture. Repeat the layers twice.
5. 5Cover and cook on LOW until the potatoes are tender, about 6 to 7 hours. (Insert a paring knife

into the center of potatoes. If it goes in and comes out easily, they are finished.) Turn off the slow cooker and uncover. Let the potatoes cool and thicken for 20 minutes before serving. Garnish with black pepper and more thyme.

6. Tip: Allow the potatoes to cool slightly before serving so the creamy cheese sauce has a chance to set up and the dish won't be too soupy.

Sweetcorn & Smoked Haddock Chowder

Servings: 2
Cooking Time: 20 Minutes

Ingredients:

- knob of butter
- 2 rashers of streaky bacon, copped
- 1 onion, finely chopped
- 500ml milk
- 350g potato (about 2 medium) cut into small cubes
- 300g frozen smoked haddock fillets (about 2)
- 140g frozen sweetcorn
- chopped parsley, to serve
- Method
- Heat the butter in a large saucepan. Tip in the bacon, then cook until starting to brown. Add the onion, cook until soft, then pour over the milk and stir through the potatoes. Bring to the boil, then simmer for 5 mins.
- Add the haddock, then leave to gently cook for another 10 mins. By now the fish should have defrosted so you can break it into large chunks. Stir through the sweetcorn, then cook for another few mins until the fish is cooked through and the sweetcorn has defrosted. Scatter over parsley, if using. Serve with plenty of crusty bread.
- RECIPE TIPS
- IF YOU WANT TO USE A SLOW COOKER...
- Heat the butter in a frying pan and cook the bacon, potatoes and onions until the onions are soft. Scrape into your slow-cooker, cover with milk and cook on High until the potatoes are soft- about 3 hours. Stir in the sweetcorn and sit the fish on top-

cover and cook for another 20-30 mins until the fish flakes easily.

Slow-cooker Puttanesca Squid

Servings: 4
Cooking Time: 3 Hours 10 Minutes

Ingredients:

- 2 tsp olive oil
- 1 onion, finely chopped
- 3 garlic cloves, crushed or finely grated
- 6 anchovy fillets
- large pinch of chilli flakes (optional)
- 1 tsp dried oregano
- 400g can cherry tomatoes or chopped tomatoes
- 600g prepared squid, tubes cut into rings, plus tentacles
- 3 tbsp capers, drained
- 150g pitted black olives
- 125ml white wine (or use water)
- small handful of parsley, finely chopped
- crusty bread, to serve (optional)

Directions:

1. Heat the oil in a frying pan over a medium heat and fry the onion for 6-8 mins until soft and beginning to brown. Add the garlic and anchovies and cook for 1 min more before scattering in the chilli, if using, and the oregano. Cook for 30 seconds, then tip into the slow cooker.

2. Pour in the can of tomatoes, then swill out the can using 1 tbsp water and pour this into the slow cooker. Add the squid, capers and olives. Pour in the white wine and give everything a good stir. Cook on high for 3 hrs until the sauce has thickened a little (it will be soup-like). Serve in bowls with the chopped parsley scattered over and some crusty bread for dunking.

3. Recipe tips

4. How to prepare it

5. Unless you feel confident preparing the squid yourself (including removing the ink sack), it's best to get it pre-prepared from your fishmonger or a fish counter. It's still worth checking that there isn't a beak left in the squid – this will feel like a piece of

plastic, and can easily be popped out. Finally, give it a good wash and drain well.

6. How to use it
7. Squid tastes best when it's either quickly fried or left to cook for a long time.

Warm Chickpea, Chorizo And Prawn Salad

Servings: 4
Cooking Time: 5 Hours 30 Minutes

Ingredients:
- 210g (1 cup) dried chickpeas
- 750ml (3 cups) Massel Salt-reduced Chicken style Liquid Stock
- 1 gluten-free chorizo sausage, sliced
- 500g green prawns, peeled, deveined, tails intact
- 1 red capsicum, deseeded, cut into thin strips
- 350g mixed cherry tomatoes, halved
- 1 small red onion, thinly sliced into rounds
- 2 tbsp extra virgin olive oil
- 1 1/2 tbsp red wine vinegar
- 1 small radicchio
- 1/3 cup fresh continental parsley leaves

Directions:
1. Combine the chickpeas and stock in a slow cooker. Cover and cook on Low for 5 hours.
2. Heat a small frying pan over medium heat and cook the chorizo for 1-2 minutes each side, until golden brown. Drain on paper towel. Add chorizo and prawns to slow cooker (lift and replace lid as quickly as possible). Cook on Low for a further 30 minutes.
3. Use a slotted spoon to transfer the chickpeas, prawns and chorizo to a large bowl. Add the capsicum, tomato and onion. Drizzle with oil and vinegar. Season.
4. Separate the radicchio leaves and arrange on a large serving platter. Top with chickpea mixture and sprinkle with parsley.

Slow-cooker Shrimp Boil

Servings: 6-8

Ingredients:
- 1/4 cup seafood seasoning, such as Old Bay
- 2 large ears yellow corn, husked and cut in to 1-inch pieces
- 1 1/2 pounds large, deveined, shell-on shrimp
- 8 ounces kielbasa, halved lengthwise and cut into 2-inch pieces
- 3 cloves garlic, lightly smashed
- 2 bay leaves
- 2 medium yellow onions, cut into eighths
- 1/2 cup chopped fresh parsley
- 1/4 cup fresh lemon juice
- Crusty bread, for serving
- 3 pounds very small red bliss potatoes

Directions:
1. Put the potatoes, garlic, bay leaves, onions, 2 tablespoons of the seafood seasoning and 4 cups water in the insert of a 6-quart slow cooker. Stir to combine. Cover with a lid and cook on low heat for 4 hours.
2. Remove the lid and switch to high heat. Gently stir in the corn, shrimp, sausage and the remaining 2 tablespoons seafood seasoning. Cover with a lid and cook until the shrimp turn opaque and the sausage is warm through, 30 to 45 minutes. Gently stir in the parsley and lemon juice.
3. Serve directly from the slow cooker or pour into a large serving bowl and serve immediately with crusty bread.

Slow-roasted Salmon With Potato Salad & Dill & Mustard Mayonnaise

Servings: 8-10
Cooking Time: 1 Hours

Ingredients:
- 1 lemon, finely sliced
- small bunch of thyme
- reserved dill stalks

- side of salmon (about 1-1.2kg), cut from the tail end
- 1 tbsp olive oil
- For the potatoes
- 1 ½ kg new potatoes, halved if large
- 1 tbsp Dijon mustard
- 1 lemon juiced
- 3 tbsp olive oil
- For the dill & mustard mayonnaise
- 200g mayonnaise
- 1 tbsp wholegrain or Dijon mustard
- small bunch of dill, leaves picked, stalks reserved

Directions:

1. Heat the oven to 120C/100C fan/gas ½. Scatter the lemon slices, thyme sprigs and reserved dill stalks over the base of a large, shallow roasting tin or baking tray. Season the salmon generously with salt and pepper and rub half the olive oil all over the fish. Lay the salmon skin-side up on top of the lemon and herbs. Roast for 45-50 mins until the fish feels firm and a corner of skin peels away easily. If you have a digital thermometer, the salmon should be at about 55C when ready. Leave to cool slightly in the tin.

2. While the salmon is cooking, tip the potatoes into a pan of cold salted water and bring to the boil. Reduce the heat to a simmer and cook for 10-15 mins until just tender. Drain. Mix the mustard, lemon juice and olive oil together in a large bowl, and season with salt and pepper. Tip the hot potatoes into the bowl and toss to coat in the dressing. Set aside. Can be served hot or made a day ahead and chilled.

3. Carefully lift the salmon onto a serving platter, if you like (it can also be served directly from the tin). Peel away and discard the skin, then use a cutlery knife to neatly scrape away the grey meat on top (see quick fishcakes recipe, below, to use it up), leaving the pink flesh underneath. The salmon is now ready to eat warm, or leave to cool completely and eat at room temperature. (See tip for garnishing the salmon, below.) Will keep chilled for up to two days. Can be served cold.

4. For the mayonnaise, mix all of the ingredients together in a small bowl. Can be made a day ahead and kept chilled. Just before serving, brush the rest of the olive oil over the salmon and season with sea salt. Serve with the potato salad and dill & mustard mayonnaise on the side.

5. Recipe tips

6. EASY MAYONNAISE

7. If you want to have a go at making your own mayonnaise, tip 2 egg yolks and 1 tbsp Dijon mustard into a jug, then pour over 250ml sunflower oil. Blitz with a hand blender, moving it up and down until the mixture has emulsified and thickened. Season. Add 1 tsp white wine vinegar or lemon juice and whizz again.

8. QUICK FISHCAKES

9. Mix any grey meat scraped off the salmon with 300g potatoes, cooked and smashed, and 1 egg, beaten. Shape into fishcakes, coat in flour and fry in sunflower oil until golden.

10. GARNISHING THE SALMON

11. If you like, brush the salmon lightly with Dijon mustard, then scatter with a small handful of dill (or use parsley or a mixture). You could also garnish with cucumber or lemon slices.

12. GRIDDLED ASPARAGUS

13. Make the most of the end of asparagus season with this side. Toss 20 asparagus spears in a drizzle of olive oil. Cook in a hot griddle pan over a medium-high heat for 10 mins until charred all over, then dress in olive oil and lemon juice, or simply toss with the potatoes.

14. ETON MESS STATION

15. For a sweet treat for a crowd, make an Eton mess station. Put crushed mini meringues in one bowl, sweetened whipped cream in another and chopped strawberries in a third alongside a stack of serving bowls for everyone to dig in.

DESSERT RECIPES

Barley And Oat Choc Chip Cookies

Servings: 12
Cooking Time: 25 Minutes

Ingredients:

- 1/4 cup extra virgin olive oil
- 1/4 cup maple syrup
- 1 egg large free-range
- 1 tsp mixed spice
- 1 tsp vanilla bean paste
- 1/4 tsp bicarbonate of soda
- 2 cups Barley+ Freedom Foods traditional barley & oat porridge
- 1 cup wholemeal flour
- 1/4 cup low fat milk
- 80 g dark chocolate chopped into pieces

Directions:

1. Preheat the oven to 180°C. Line a baking tray with baking paper.
2. In a food processor blend the extra virgin olive oil, maple syrup and egg.
3. Add the mixed spice, vanilla bean paste, bicarb soda, 1 cup of barley & oats porridge, the flour and the milk. Process for 30 seconds or so to combine.
4. Transfer to a mixing bowl and stir through the second cup of barley & oats and the dark chocolate chips. If the mixture is too thick add a splash more of milk.
5. Using an ice-cream scoop, spoon portions of the cookie mixture onto the prepared tray and flatten slightly to form a rough cookie shape.
6. Bake in the oven for 20 minutes or until lightly golden and cooked through.
7. Remove from the oven and allow to cool completely on the tray. Once cooled the cookies will keep in an airtight container for 3-4 days.

Easy Chocolate Fudge Cake

Servings: 8
Cooking Time: 30 Minutes

Ingredients:

- 150ml sunflower oil, plus extra for the tin
- 175g self-raising flour
- 2 tbsp cocoa powder
- 1 tsp bicarbonate of soda
- 150g caster sugar
- 2 tbsp golden syrup
- 2 large eggs, lightly beaten
- 150ml semi-skimmed milk
- For the icing
- 100g unsalted butter
- 225g icing sugar
- 40g cocoa powder
- 2½ tbsp milk (a little more if needed)

Directions:

1. Heat the oven to 180C/160C fan/gas 4. Oil and line the base of two 18cm sandwich tins. Sieve the flour, cocoa powder and bicarbonate of soda into a bowl. Add the caster sugar and mix well.
2. Make a well in the centre and add the golden syrup, eggs, sunflower oil and milk. Beat well with an electric whisk until smooth.
3. Pour the mixture into the two tins and bake for 25-30 mins until risen and firm to the touch. Remove from oven, leave to cool for 10 mins before turning out onto a cooling rack.
4. To make the icing, beat the unsalted butter in a bowl until soft. Gradually sieve and beat in the icing sugar and cocoa powder, then add enough of the milk to make the icing fluffy and spreadable.
5. Sandwich the two cakes together with the butter icing and cover the sides and the top of the cake with more icing.

Slow Cooker Apple Crumble Recipe

Servings: 4
Cooking Time: 3 Hours 30 Minutes

Ingredients:

- 5 Granny Smith apples, peeled, cored and each cut into 8 wedges
- 1 tsp ground cinnamon
- 1 orange, zested and half juiced
- 60g rolled oats
- 50g walnut pieces
- ½ tsp ground ginger
- 75g plain flour
- 85g light muscovado sugar
- 90g unsalted butter, melted

Directions:

1. Put the slices of apple in a slow cooker. Sprinkle over the ground cinnamon, orange zest and 1 tbsp juice and mix together.
2. Put the oats and walnuts into a food processor and pulse a few times to give the texture of very course breadcrumbs. Pour into a bowl.
3. Stir the ginger, flour and sugar into the oat and walnut mixture then add the butter and mix well.
4. Spoon the crumble mix over the apples, covering them all. Lay two sheets of kitchen paper or kitchen roll on top of the crumble. Cover with the slow cooker lid and cook on a low heat for 3½ hrs.
5. Remove the kitchen paper and cook for the last 10 mins with the lid just slightly ajar.
6. Tip: Laying kitchen roll on top of the crumble helps prevent condensation dripping back onto the crumble, so you get a more crisp crust.

Lemon & Poppyseed Cupcakes

Servings: 12
Cooking Time: 22 Minutes

Ingredients:

- 225g self-raising flour
- 175g golden caster sugar
- zest 2 lemons
- 1 tbsp poppy seeds, toasted
- 3 eggs
- 100g natural yogurt
- 175g butter, melted and cooled a little
- For the icing
- 225g butter, softened
- 400g icing sugar, sifted
- juice 1 lemon
- few drops yellow food colouring
- icing flowers or yellow sprinkles, to decorate

Directions:

1. Heat oven to 180C/160C fan/gas 4 and line a 12-hole muffin tin with cupcake or muffin cases. Mix the flour, sugar, lemon zest and poppy seeds together in a large mixing bowl. Beat the eggs into the yogurt, then tip this into the dry ingredients with the melted butter. Mix together with a wooden spoon or whisk until lump-free, then divide between the cases. Bake for 20-22 mins until a skewer poked in comes out clean – the cakes will be quite pale on top still. Cool for 5 mins in the tin, then carefully lift onto a wire rack to finish cooling.
2. To ice, beat the softened butter until really soft in a large bowl, then gradually beat in the icing sugar and lemon juice. Stir in enough food colouring for a pale lemon colour, then spoon the icing into a piping bag with a large star nozzle.
3. Ice one cake at a time, holding the piping bag almost upright with the nozzle about 1cm from the surface of the cake. Pipe one spiral of icing around the edge, then pause to break the flow before moving the nozzle towards the centre slightly and piping a second, smaller spiral that continues until there are no gaps in the centre. Slightly 'dot' the nozzle into the icing as you stop squeezing to finish

neatly. Repeat to cover all the cakes, then top with sugar decorations or scatter with sprinkles.

Apricot And White Chocolate Chip Biscuits

Servings: 24
Cooking Time: 10 Minutes

Ingredients:
- 1 cup plain flour
- 1/4 tsp bicarbonate of soda
- 1/2 cup brown sugar
- 1/4 cup caster sugar
- 1 cup rolled oats
- 200g Turkish dried apricots chopped
- 125g white chocolate chips
- 1 egg
- 125g butter melted

Directions:
1. Preheat over to 180C. Line biscuit slides with baking paper.
2. Sift flour and bicarbonate of soda.
3. Add sugars, oats, apricots and chocolate and mix well.
4. Add egg and melted butter.
5. Roll about a tablespoon of mixture into balls and flatten on trays, placing the biscuits 5 cm apart.
6. Bake for 10 minutes.
7. Cool on trays.

NOTES
Makes 24 x 5cm biscuits. For larger biscuits cook a little longer.
Works well with brown rice flour to make it gluten-free.

Slow-cooker Stuffed Apples With Caramel Sauce

Servings: 4
Cooking Time: 2 Hours

Ingredients:
- 4 large Pink Lady apples
- 2/3 cup (70g) granola
- 4 fresh dates, coarsely chopped
- 1/2 tsp ground cinnamon
- 60g butter, softened
- 1/2 cup (110g) brown sugar
- 1/4 cup (60ml) thickened cream
- Double cream, to serve

Directions:
1. Use an apple corer to remove the core from each apple. Use a teaspoon to carefully cut each apple centre to make a 2.5cm-diameter wide cavity. Cut a horizontal slit around each apple (don't cut all the way through).
2. Combine granola, date, cinnamon and 20g of the butter in a small bowl. Divide the mixture evenly among the apple cavities. Place in a slow cooker. Dot the remaining butter around apples. Sprinkle with sugar and drizzle with thickened cream. Add 2/3 cup (160ml) water to the slow cooker. Cover and cook for 2 hours on high or until tender.
3. Divide apples among serving plates and spoon over the caramel sauce. Serve with double cream.

Slow Cooker Rice Pudding

Servings: 6
Cooking Time: 2hours 30 Minutes

Ingredients:
- 1 tsp butter
- 1l semi-skimmed milk
- 200g wholegrain rice
- nutmeg or cinnamon
- 1 tbsp honey, a handful toasted, flaked almonds and fruit, to serve

Directions:

1. Butter the slow cooker all over the base and half way up the sides. Heat the milk to simmering point. Mix the pudding rice with the milk and pour it into the slow cooker. Add a grating of nutmeg or cinnamon. Cook for 2½ hours on High and stir once or twice if you can.

2. Serve with honey, or flaked almonds and fruit if you like.

Classic Scones With Jam & Clotted Cream

Servings: 8
Cooking Time: 10 Minutes

Ingredients:

- 350g self-raising flour, plus more for dusting
- 1 tsp baking powder
- 85g butter, cut into cubes
- 3 tbsp caster sugar
- 175ml milk
- 1 tsp vanilla extract
- squeeze lemon juice
- beaten egg, to glaze
- jam and clotted cream, to serve

Directions:

1. Heat the oven to 220C/200C fan/gas 7. Tip the self-raising flour into a large bowl with ¼ tsp salt and the baking powder, then mix.

2. Add the butter, then rub in with your fingers until the mix looks like fine crumbs. Stir in the caster sugar.

3. Put the milk into a jug and heat in the microwave for about 30 secs until warm, but not hot. Add the vanilla extract and a squeeze of lemon juice, then set aside for a moment.

4. Put a baking tray in the oven. Make a well in the dry mix, then add the liquid and combine it quickly with a cutlery knife – it will seem pretty wet at first.

5. Scatter some flour onto the work surface and tip the dough out. Dredge the dough and your hands with a little more flour, then fold the dough over 2-3 times until it's a little smoother. Pat into a round about 4cm deep. Take a 5cm cutter (smooth-edged cutters tend to cut more cleanly, giving a better rise) and dip it into some flour. Plunge into the dough, then repeat until you have four scones. You may need to press what's left of the dough back into a round to cut out another four.

6. Brush the tops with a beaten egg, then carefully arrange on the hot baking tray. Bake for 10 mins until risen and golden on the top. Eat just warm or cold on the day of baking, generously topped with jam and clotted cream. If freezing, freeze once cool. Defrost, then put in a low oven (about 160C/140C fan/gas 3) for a few minutes to refresh.

7. RECIPE TIPS

8. KNOW-HOW

9. Adding a squeeze of lemon juice to the milk sours it slightly, mimicking sharp-tasting buttermilk, often used in scones but sometimes tricky to find. The slightly acidic mix gives a

10. boost to the raising agents in the flour and baking powder.

11. JANE SAYS...

12. Scones are so quick to make that my mum would often emerge with a plateful before we'd even noticed she'd gone! I've borrowed her tip of using warm milk, and added a few tricks of

13. my own for light scones that rise every time

14. TOWERING TALL

15. For toweringly tall scones, always pat the dough out a bit thicker than you think you should. I say pat rather than knead because scones are essentially a sweet soda bread and, like other soda breads, will become tough when over-handled. Kick-start the scones' rise with a hot baking tray and don't leave the dough sitting around. If you like your scones with lots of juicy fruit, stir 85g plump sultanas into the mix at the same time as the sugar.

Slow-cooker Cranberry-walnut Stuffed Apples

Servings: 4-6
Cooking Time: 4 Hours

Ingredients:

- 3/4 cup walnuts, toasted and chopped
- 1/2 cup chopped dried cranberries
- 1/3 cup packed light brown sugar
- 1/3 cup rolled oats
- 3 tablespoons unsalted butter, cut into small pieces
- 1 tablespoon fresh lemon juice
- 1/2 teaspoon ground cinnamon
- Kosher salt
- 4 large or 6 medium firm baking apples (such as Rome, Golden Delicious or Honey Crisp)
- 1 cup apple cider
- Vanilla ice cream and pure maple syrup, for serving

Directions:

1. Combine the walnuts, cranberries, brown sugar, oats, butter, lemon juice, cinnamon and 1/2 teaspoon salt in a small bowl and squeeze together until a wet and sandy mixture is formed.
2. Scoop the core out of each apple with a melon baller, taking care not to scoop completely through to the bottom or the sides. Stuff each apple with some of the cranberry-walnut mixture. Place the apples in the slow cooker insert and pour in the apple cider. Cover and cook on low until the apples are tender but still slightly firm, 3 to 4 hours depending on the size and type of apple. (If your apples are on the smaller size, check after 2 hours; they may cook faster.)
3. Serve each apple whole or cut in half in a bowl with a scoop of ice cream and a drizzle of maple syrup.

Easy Carrot Cake

Servings: 10-12
Cooking Time: 30 Minutes

Ingredients:

- 230ml vegetable oil, plus extra for the tin
- 100g natural yogurt
- 4 large eggs
- 1½ tsp vanilla extract
- ½ orange, zested
- 265g self-raising flour
- 335g light muscovado sugar
- 2½ tsp ground cinnamon
- ¼ fresh nutmeg, finely grated
- 265g carrots (about 3), grated
- 100g sultanas or raisins
- 100g walnuts or pecans, roughly chopped (optional)
- For the icing
- 100g slightly salted butter, softened
- 300g icing sugar
- 100g soft cheese

Directions:

1. Heat the oven to 180C/160C fan/gas 4. Oil and line the base and sides of two 20cm cake tins with baking parchment. Whisk the oil, yogurt, eggs, vanilla and zest in a jug. Mix the flour, sugar, cinnamon and nutmeg with a good pinch of salt in a bowl. Squeeze any lumps of sugar through your fingers, shaking the bowl a few times to bring the lumps to the surface.
2. Add the wet ingredients to the dry, along with the carrots, raisins and half the nuts, if using. Mix well to combine, then divide between the tins.
3. Bake for 25-30 mins or until a skewer inserted into the centre of the cake comes out clean. If any wet mixture clings to the skewer, return to the oven for 5 mins, then check again. Leave to cool in the tins.
4. To make the icing, beat the butter and sugar together until smooth. Add half the soft cheese and beat again, then add the rest (adding it bit by bit prevents the icing from splitting). Remove the cakes from the tins and sandwich together with half the icing. Top with the remaining icing and scatter

with the remaining walnuts. Will keep in the fridge for up to five days. Best eaten at room temperature.

Slow Cooker Chocolate Candy

Servings: 30-40
Cooking Time: 3 Hours

Ingredients:

- Deselect All
- 2 pounds salted dry-roasted peanuts
- 4 ounces German's sweet chocolate (about 4 squares)
- One 12-ounce package semisweet chocolate chips (about 2 cups)
- 2 1/2 pounds white almond bark

Directions:

1. Put the peanuts in the bottom of a 4-quart slow cooker. Layer the chocolate over the peanuts, beginning with the sweet chocolate, followed by the chocolate chips and then the almond bark. Set the temperature on low and cook for 3 hours. Do not stir the mixture. After 3 hours, stir the mixture with a wooden spoon until smooth. Drop the candy into cupcake pan liners using about 2 tablespoons per liner. Allow the candy to cool completely before removing the cupcake liners.

Vegan Peanut Butter Choc Chip Cookies

Servings: 12
Cooking Time: 15 Minutes

Ingredients:

- 1/2 cup coconut flour
- 2 tbs chia seeds
- 1/3 cup cashews raw
- 2 tbs peanut butter heaped
- 2 tbs maple syrup
- 1 tsp sea salt
- 1 tbs coconut oil melted
- 1/4 cup warm water
- 1/4 cup dark chocolate chopped

Directions:

1. Preheat oven to 180C.
2. Add all the Ingredients to a food processor, except for the chopped chocolate, and process until the mixture comes together. You will know when the mixture is ready, as it will be sticky enough to hold its shape when pressed. If it is too dry, add a touch more water.
3. Add the chopped chocolate and stir through.
4. Spoon 1tbs of mixture onto a lined baking tray and shape into a cookie.
5. Bake for 12-15 minutes, until golden around the edges.

NOTES

You can replace raw cashews with raw almonds if you prefer.

While most dark chocolate varieties containing over 70% cocoa are free from dairy, not all dark chocolate is suitable for vegans. Check the Ingredients before purchase.

Choc Chip Slice

Servings: 12
Cooking Time: 30 Minutes

Ingredients:

- 125 g butter cubed room temperature
- 110 g brown sugar firmly packed
- 110 g caster sugar
- 2 egg
- 1 cup plain flour
- 250 g choc bits

Directions:

1. Preheat oven to 180C and line the base of slice pan with baking paper.
2. Using electric beaters, beat the butter and sugars until light and creamy.
3. Add eggs and beat until combined.
4. Sift flour over the butter mixture and mix together until just combined.
5. Add the choc bits and mix until evenly combined.
6. Spoon mixture into pan and spread evenly.
7. Bake for 30 minutes or until firm to touch.
8. Remove and set aside to cool, then cut evenly into pieces.

Slow Cooker Gooey Brownie Cake

Servings: 6-8
Cooking Time: 3 Hours

Ingredients:

- 1 1/2 sticks unsalted butter, melted, plus more for greasing insert
- 1 1/2 cups sugar
- 2/3 cup unsweetened cocoa powder
- 1/3 cup all-purpose flour
- 3 large eggs, lightly beaten
- 1 teaspoon pure vanilla extract
- Kosher salt
- 1/2 cup semisweet chocolate chunks
- Vanilla ice cream, for serving

Directions:

1. Line the insert of a 4- or 6-quart slow cooker with a large piece of foil, then generously butter the foil.
2. Whisk together the melted butter, sugar, cocoa powder, flour, eggs, vanilla and 1/2 teaspoon salt in a medium bowl. Fold in the chocolate chunks. Scrape the batter out into the prepared insert in an even layer. Cover and cook on low for 3 hours; the cake should be set around the edges and gooey in the center.
3. Serve the cake warm, scooped into a bowl and topped with ice cream.

Pear, Berry And White Chocolate Cobbler

Servings: 6
Cooking Time: 3 Hours

Ingredients:

- 4 pears, peeled, cored, cut into wedges
- 300g Coles Frozen Mixed Berries
- 1/3 cup (75g) caster sugar
- 1/4 cup (35g) plain flour
- 1 tsp vanilla bean paste
- 1 1/2 cup (225g) self-raising flour
- 1 tbsp caster sugar, extra
- 120g butter, chopped
- 3/4 cup (185ml) buttermilk
- 100g white chocolate, chopped
- Vanilla ice cream, to serve

Directions:

1. Combine the pear, berries, sugar, plain flour and vanilla in a slow cooker. Set aside for 20 mins or until the berries begin to release their juices.
2. Combine self-raising flour and extra sugar in a large bowl. Add butter. Use your fingertips to rub the butter into the flour mixture until it resembles fine breadcrumbs. Make a well in the centre and pour in buttermilk. Stir until a soft, sticky dough forms. Stir in chocolate.
3. Spoon the chocolate mixture evenly over the pear mixture in slow cooker. Cover and cook on high for 3 hours or until the top is cooked through and the fruit is tender. Serve with ice cream.

NOTES

Any type of frozen or fresh berries will do. Apples work in place of pears in this dish too.

Slow Cooker Baked Apples

Servings: 4

Ingredients:

- 6 tbsp. butter, softened
- 1/4 c. chopped pecans
- 1/4 c. old-fashioned oats
- 1/4 c. brown sugar
- 1 tsp. ground cinnamon
- 1/4 tsp. ground ginger
- Pinch kosher salt
- 4 apples
- FOR SERVING
- Ice cream
- Caramel, warmed

Directions:

1. In a large bowl, mix together butter, pecans, oats, brown sugar, cinnamon, ginger, and salt.
2. Slice off top of each apple and use a melon baller to scoop out core.

3. Stuff butter mixture into apples, then place in slow cooker.
4. Cook until apples are tender, on high for about 2 hours or on low for about 5 hours. Serve warm with ice cream and caramel.

Sweetened Condensed Milk Caramel

Servings: 3
Cooking Time: 8 Hours

Ingredients:

- 2 cans sweetened condensed milk (395g / 14 oz each)
- Instructions
- Place cans in slow cooker on their side. Don't worry about removing the label.
- Cover cans with hot tap water until the water is about 5 cm / 2" above the cans.
- Set slow cooker for 8 hours on low.
- If you want your caramel to be a really dark golden colour, slow cook for a further 2 hours.
- Remove cans from slow cooker using tongs. DO NOT OPEN CANS WHILE HOT. The contents might burst out – dangerous!
- Submerge cans in cold water to cool before opening. It only takes 10 minutes or so.
- Open cans.
- If not using right away, transfer into jars or air tight containers, do not leave it in the can.
- To make on stove top
- Place cans in a large pot and cover with water so that it is 5 cm / 2 inches above the cans.
- Place on a small burner and bring JUST to boil - don't walk away, you don't want to leave the cans boiling in water.
- Then turn down the heat to medium low (or low if you stove is powerful), put the lid on and let it simmer for 2 hours to get the consistency and colour as per the photos you see, otherwise for 3 hours if you want to darker and thicker.
- Remove from the pot. Allow to cool before opening (otherwise the Dulce De Leche might burst out when you open it). You can speed up the process by submerging the cans in cold water.

NOTES

You must use sweetened condensed milk, not evaporated milk. It won't work with evaporated milk.

If your slow cooker leaks a lot of water, you should increase the water quantity. If the water dries out during cooking, the cans might burst open.

The Dulce De Leche will keep in the fridge for up to 1 month.

When the Dulce De Leche is warmed, it becomes pourable like a thick caramel. At room temperature or fridge cold, it is thicker, like a spread.

You can use a touch of water or milk to thin it out slightly if you want to drizzle it over something.

Suggestions for use: As a sweetener + milk in coffee• Use as spread on muffins, toast or graham crackers• Drizzled over cakes and cupcakes. Fancy!• Caramel layer in slices• Over crepes and pancakes• Cheesecake• As a dip for churros (it is, after all, South American!)• As a gift – jar it and add labels and/or tags

Choc Chip Muffins

Servings: 20
Cooking Time: 25 Minutes

Ingredients:

- 3 cups self-raising flour
- 3 tbs cocoa powder
- 1 1/2 cups brown sugar
- 200 g choc bits
- 1 1/2 cups milk
- 120g butter, melted
- 2 eggs beaten

Directions:

1. Sift flour and cocoa.
2. This is a modal window.
3. Add sugar and choc chips, stir.
4. Add milk, butter and eggs. Stir until just combined.
5. Spoon into muffin tin ¾ full.
6. Bake at 180C for 20-25 minutes.

NOTES

These are also nice with walnuts or white choc chips in them.

Slow-cooker Chai Hot Chocolate

Servings: 8
Cooking Time: 1hours

Ingredients:

- 1 cinnamon stick or quill
- 2 whole star anise
- 4 whole cloves
- 1 tsp ground ginger
- 1 tsp ground cardamom
- 1/2 tsp freshly ground fennel seeds
- 1/2 tsp ground allspice
- Freshly ground black pepper
- 8 cups (2L) milk
- 400g dark chocolate, finely chopped
- Whipped cream, to serve
- Ground cinnamon, to serve

Directions:

1. Cook the cinnamon stick or quill, star anise, cloves, ginger, cardamom, fennel and allspice in a small frying pan over high heat, stirring, for 30 secs on until aromatic. Transfer to a slow cooker. Season with pepper. Add the milk and chocolate. Cook on low, stirring occasionally, for 1 hour or until mixture is smooth and heated through.
2. Divide among serving glasses. Top with whipped cream and sprinkle with chocolate and cinnamon.

NOTES

Cook's Note:
For a classic hot choc finish, top with finely grated chocolate and white and pink mini marshmallows.

Double Chocolate Loaf Cake

Servings: 8-10
Cooking Time: 55 Minutes

Ingredients:

- 175g softened butter, plus extra for greasing
- 175g golden caster sugar
- 3 eggs
- 140g self-raising flour
- 85g ground almonds
- 1/2 tsp baking powder
- 100ml milk
- 4 tbsp cocoa powder
- 50g plain chocolate chip or chunks
- few extra chunks white, plain and milk chocolate, for decorating

Directions:

1. Heat oven to 160C/140C fan/gas 3. Grease and line a 2lb/900g loaf tin with a long strip of baking parchment. To make the loaf cake batter, beat the butter and sugar with an electric whisk until light and fluffy. Beat in the eggs, flour, almonds, baking powder, milk and cocoa until smooth. Stir in the chocolate chips, then scrape into the tin. Bake for 45-50 mins until golden, risen and a skewer poked in the centre comes out clean.
2. Cool in the tin, then lift out onto a wire rack over some kitchen paper. Melt the extra chocolate chunks separately in pans over barely simmering water, or in bowls in the microwave, then use a spoon to drizzle each in turn over the cake. Leave to set before slicing.

Slow-cooker Cherry Buckle

Servings: 8
Cooking Time: 3 Hours

Ingredients:

- 2 cans (15 ounces each) sliced pears, drained
- 1 can (21 ounces) cherry pie filling
- 1/4 teaspoon almond extract
- 1 package yellow cake mix (regular size)
- 1/4 cup old-fashioned oats
- 1/4 cup sliced almonds
- 1 tablespoon brown sugar
- 1/2 cup butter, melted
- Vanilla ice cream, optional

Directions:

1. In a greased 5-qt. slow cooker, combine pears and pie filling; stir in extract. In a large bowl, combine cake mix, oats, almonds and brown sugar; stir in melted butter. Sprinkle over fruit.

2. Cook, covered, on low until topping is golden brown, 3-4 hours. If desired, serve with ice cream.

Slow Cooker Fudge

Servings:
Cooking Time: 1 Hours

Ingredients:

- 375g can condensed milk
- 250g milk chocolate, chopped
- 250g dark chocolate, chopped
- 100g light brown soft sugar
- 1 tsp vanilla extract
- vegetable oil, for the tin

Directions:

1. Set the slow cooker to low (we used a 6-litre cooker). Tip in the condensed milk, both chocolates, the sugar, vanilla and a pinch of salt. Cook for 1 hr, stirring well with a spatula every 15 mins to combine and scrape off any bits that start to stick to the bowl, until thick and smooth. Oil a 20cm square tin, then line with baking parchment. Pour the fudge mixture into the tin and chill for 4 hrs.
2. Cut the fudge into 36 squares using a sharp knife. Will keep in an airtight container in the fridge for three days.

Slow Cooker Spiced Apples With Barley

Servings: 4
Cooking Time: 2 Hours

Ingredients:

- ½ cup barley
- 2 eating apples
- ½ tsp cinnamon
- a grating of fresh nutmeg
- finely grated zest 1 large orange
- 4 tbsp natural yogurt

Directions:

1. Heat the slow cooker if necessary. Put the barley and 750ml boiling water into the slow cooker. Peel and core the apples so you have a hole the size of a pound coin in each one. Cut each apple in half.
2. Stand the apples skin side down on the barley. Mix the cinnamon, nutmeg and orange zest, and sprinkle them over the apples.
3. Cook on Low for 2 hours. Serve with natural yogurt.

Chocolate Cupcakes

Servings: 12
Cooking Time: 20 Minutes - 25minutes

Ingredients:

- 100g plain flour
- 20g cocoa powder
- 140g caster sugar
- 1½ tsp baking powder
- 40g unsalted butter (at room temperature)
- 120ml whole milk
- 1 egg
- ¼ tsp vanilla extract
- To decorate
- buttercream
- chocolate vermicelli (optional)

Directions:

1. Heat oven to 180C/160C fan/gas 4. Put the flour, cocoa powder, sugar, baking powder, a pinch of salt and the butter in a free-standing electric mixer with a paddle attachment (or use a handheld electric whisk). Beat on a slow speed until you get a sandy consistency and everything is combined.
2. Whisk the milk, egg and vanilla extract together in a jug, then slowly pour about half into the flour mixture. Beat to combine and turn the mixer up to high speed, scraping any mixture from the side of the bowl with a rubber spatula. Pour in the remaining liquid and continue mixing for a couple more minutes until the mixture is smooth. Do not overmix.
3. Spoon the mixture into the paper cases until approximately two-thirds full. Bake in a preheated oven for 20-25 minutes, or until the sponge bounces back when touched and a skewer inserted into the centre comes out clean.

4. Leave the cupcakes to cool slightly in the tray before turning out onto a wire cooling rack to cool completely. Meanwhile, make chocolate buttercream or plain buttercream and spread it over the cakes with a palette knife, or use a piping bag. Scatter over chocolate vermicelli, if you like.

Amazing Slow-cooker Mulled Wine

Servings: 6
Cooking Time: 4hours 5 Minutes

Ingredients:
- 250ml (1 cup) pulp-free orange juice
- 55g (1/4 cup) caster sugar
- 3 whole star anise
- 2 cinnamon sticks, plus extra, to serve (optional)
- 5 cardamom pods
- 5 cloves
- 1/4 tsp fennel seeds
- 750ml bottle fruity red wine (see **NOTES**)
- 3-4 strips orange rind
- 1 orange, thinly sliced
- Pomegranate seeds, to serve

Directions:
1. Combine the orange juice, sugar, star anise, cinnamon, cardamom, cloves and fennel seeds in a small saucepan. Bring to the boil over high heat, stirring to dissolve the sugar. Transfer to a slow cooker.
2. Add the red wine and orange rind to the slow cooker. Cover and cook for 4 hours on high heat.
3. Pour into heatproof glasses and serve with slices of fresh orange and pomegranate seeds.

NOTES
Use a pinot noir, Sangiovese or merlot.

Slow-cooker Poached Cinnamon And Vanilla Quinces

Servings: 4
Cooking Time: 10 Hours

Ingredients:
- 1 cup caster sugar
- 1 vanilla bean, split
- 1 cinnamon stick
- 1 whole cloves
- 3 (180g each) quince
- Double cream, to serve

Directions:
1. Place sugar and 1 litre cold water in a saucepan over low heat. Cook, stirring occasionally, for 5 minutes or until sugar dissolves. Increase heat to medium. Bring to the boil. Remove from heat. Carefully pour sugar syrup into the bowl of a 5.5-litre slow cooker. Add vanilla bean, cinnamon and clove.
2. One at a time, peel, quarter and core quince and place immediately into sugar syrup (see note). Cover with lid. Cook on low for 10 hours or on high for 6 hours until quince is tender and deep red in colour. Serve quince drizzled with syrup and dolloped with double cream.

NOTES
The cut quince will turn brown when exposed to the air, so you will need to work quickly.

To cook this recipe in the oven, preheat to 180C/160C fan-forced. Combine all Ingredients with 1 litre cold water in a deep baking dish. Cover surface with baking paper, then cover dish tightly with foil. Bake for 3 hours or until tender.

SOUPS AND STEWS RECIPES

Easy Slow Cooker Butternut Squash Soup

Servings: 6

Ingredients:

- 1 large butternut squash, peeled and cut into large cubes (about 8 cups)
- 1 large onion, chopped
- 1 carrot, peeled and chopped
- 3 cloves garlic, minced
- 4 sprigs thyme
- 1 sprig sage
- 3 c. low-sodium chicken (or vegetable) broth
- Kosher salt
- Freshly ground black pepper
- Pinch of cayenne
- Heavy cream, for serving
- Freshly chopped parsley, for garnish

Directions:

1. In a large slow cooker, combine butternut squash, onion, carrot, garlic, thyme, and sage. Pour in broth and season with salt, pepper, and a pinch of cayenne.
2. Cover and cook until squash is very tender, on low for 8 hours or on high for 4 hours. Remove herb sprigs and use an immersion blender to blend soup until smooth.
3. Stir in cream and garnish with parsley before serving.

Chicken Mushroom Stew

Servings: 6
Cooking Time: 4 Hours

Ingredients:

- 6 boneless skinless chicken breast halves (4 ounces each)
- 2 tablespoons canola oil, divided
- 8 ounces fresh mushrooms, sliced
- 1 medium onion, diced
- 3 cups diced zucchini
- 1 cup chopped green pepper
- 4 garlic cloves, minced
- 3 medium tomatoes, chopped
- 1 can (6 ounces) tomato paste
- 3/4 cup water
- 2 teaspoons each dried thyme, oregano, marjoram, and basil
- Chopped fresh thyme, optional

Directions:

1. Cut chicken into 1-in. cubes; brown in 1 tablespoon oil in a large skillet. Transfer to a 3-qt. slow cooker. In the same skillet, saute the mushrooms, onion, zucchini and green pepper in remaining 1 Tbsp. oil until crisp-tender; add garlic; cook 1 minute longer.
2. Place in slow cooker. Add the tomatoes, tomato paste, water and seasonings. Cover and cook on low for 4-5 hours or until the meat is no longer pink and vegetables are tender. If desired, top with chopped fresh thyme.

Beef Stew

Servings: 5
Cooking Time: 3 Hours-3 Hours 50 Minutes

Ingredients:

- 2 celery sticks, thickly sliced
- 1 onion, chopped
- 2 really big carrots, halved lengthways then very chunkily sliced
- 5 bay leaves
- 2 thyme sprigs, 1 whole and 1 leaves picked
- 1 tbsp vegetable oil
- 1 tbsp butter
- 2 tbsp plain flour
- 2 tbsp tomato purée
- 2 tbsp Worcestershire sauce

- 2 beef stock cubes, crumbled
- 850g stewing beef (featherblade or brisket works nicely), cut into nice large chunks

Directions:

1. Heat oven to 160C/140C fan/gas 3 and put the kettle on.
2. Put 2 thickly sliced celery sticks, 1 chopped onion, 2 chunkily sliced carrots, 5 bay leaves and 1 whole thyme sprig in a flameproof casserole dish with 1 tbsp vegetable oil and 1 tbsp butter.
3. Soften for 10 mins, then stir in 2 tbsp plain flour until it doesn't look dusty anymore, followed by 2 tbsp tomato purée, 2 tbsp Worcestershire sauce and 2 crumbled beef stock cubes.
4. Gradually stir in 600ml hot water, then tip in 850g stewing beef and bring to a gentle simmer.
5. Cover and put in the oven for 2hrs 30 mins, then uncover and cook for 30mins – 1hr more until the meat is really tender and the sauce is thickened.
6. Garnish with the picked leaves of the remaining thyme sprig.

Slow-cooker Chipotle Chicken Stew

Servings: 4
Cooking Time: 7 Hours 30 Minutes

Ingredients:

- 1 1/4 pounds skinless, boneless chicken thighs, cut into 2-inch pieces
- 2 teaspoons ground cumin
- Kosher salt and freshly ground pepper
- 1 onion, chopped
- 1 15-ounce can diced fire-roasted tomatoes with green chiles
- 1 chipotle chile in adobo sauce, seeded and chopped, plus 1 tablespoon sauce from the can
- 1/2 teaspoon dried oregano
- 1 cup frozen corn (preferably fire-roasted), thawed
- 8 corn tortillas
- 1/4 cup crumbled Cotija cheese
- 1 avocado, diced

- 1/2 cup fresh cilantro, torn

Directions:

1. Put the chicken in a 6- to 8-quart slow cooker and sprinkle with 1 teaspoon cumin, 1/2 teaspoon salt and a few grinds of pepper. Add the onion, tomatoes, chipotle and adobo sauce, oregano, the remaining 1 teaspoon cumin and 1/2 teaspoon salt. Cover and cook on low until the chicken is tender and the sauce is slightly thickened, about 7 1/2 hours. Add the corn and stir until warmed through.
2. Warm the tortillas in a dry skillet or in the microwave. Top each serving of stew with cheese, avocado and cilantro. Serve with the warm tortillas.

Beef, Beetroot And Butter Bean Stew With Stilton Dumplings Recipe

Servings: 8
Cooking Time: 3 Hours

Ingredients:

- 2 tbsp plain flour
- ½ tsp ground allspice
- 600g beef casserole steak, diced
- 3 tbsp vegetable oil
- 2 carrots, peeled and roughly chopped
- 2 celery sticks, roughly chopped
- 2 parsnips, peeled and roughly chopped
- 400g pack shallots, peeled but kept whole; 2 reserved and finely chopped
- 450g raw beetroot, peeled and cut into thick wedges
- 4 garlic cloves, finely chopped
- 10 sprigs thyme
- 150ml red wine
- 1 litre of beef stock, made using OXO Beef Cubes
- 1 tbsp tomato purée
- 2 bay leaves
- 400g tin butter beans, drained
- For the dumplings
- 125g self-raising flour

- 3 thyme sprigs, leaves removed and chopped
- 50g suet, grated
- 60g Stilton, roughly crumbled
- For the green beans
- 3 x 220g packs green beans, trimmed
- ½ tbsp olive oil
- 1 garlic clove, finely chopped
- 1 tsp Dijon mustard
- 1 tbsp white wine vinegar

Directions:

1. Season the plain flour with the allspice, salt and pepper. Mix thoroughly, then coat the beef. Heat 1 tbsp oil in a large casserole dish on a medium-high heat and cook half of the beef for 2-3 mins, stirring once or twice, until golden. Remove and set aside, then repeat with 1 tbsp oil and the remaining beef. If there are lots of bits stuck to the bottom of the dish, add a little water and keep it on the heat, stirring and scraping, until loosened, then pour off and reserve.

2. Preheat the oven to gas 3, 170°C, fan 150°C. Add the remaining oil to the dish and gently fry the carrots, celery, parsnips and whole shallots for 10 mins, until golden and starting to soften. Stir in the beetroot, garlic and thyme and cook for 2 mins, stirring, before adding the beef, red wine, stock, tomato purée, bay leaves and any reserved water from step 1. Bring to the boil then cover and put in the oven to cook for 2 hrs 15 mins.

3. Meanwhile, to make the dumplings, put the flour and thyme in a bowl with the suet and Stilton; season, then mix together. Pour in 3-4 tbsp of water, a tablespoon at a time, and stir in quickly with a knife to form a dough. Shape the dough into 12 walnut-sized balls.

4. Remove the beef from the oven and turn the temperature up to gas 4, 180°C, fan 160°C. Stir in the butter beans, put the dumplings on top, then return to the oven for 20 mins, until the dumplings are cooked through, the beef is tender and the sauce is thick.

5. Meanwhile, prepare the green beans. Bring a large pan of water to the boil and cook the beans for 4 minutes. Drain, reserving a little of the cooking water. Heat the olive oil in a pan over a medium heat then add the chopped shallots and garlic and cook for 5 mins, until softened. Add the mustard, vinegar and 2 tbsp of the reserved cooking water and bring to the boil. Stir in the green beans and toss together until combined. Serve immediately with the stew and dumplings, discarding the thyme and bay leaves.

6. Tip: Try swapping the Stilton for 2 tbsp creamed horseradish.

7. Freezing and defrosting guidelines

8. Freeze the stew only. Once the cooked dish has cooled completely, transfer it to an airtight, freezer-safe container, seal and freeze for up to 1 month. To serve, defrost overnight before reheating thoroughly.

Beef And Guinness Stew

Servings: 6
Cooking Time: 3 Hours

Ingredients:

- 2 tbsp olive oil
- 2.5 lb / 1.25 kg beef chuck , boneless short rib or any other slow cooking beef
- 3/4 tsp each salt and black pepper
- 3 garlic cloves , minced
- 2 onions , chopped (brown, white or yellow)
- 6 oz / 180g bacon , speck or pancetta, diced
- 3 tbsp flour (all purpose/plain, Note 3 for GF)
- 440ml / 14.9 oz Guinness Beer
- 4 tbsp tomato paste
- 3 cups (750 ml) chicken stock/broth
- 3 carrots , peeled and cut into 1.25 cm / 1/2" thick pieces
- 2 large celery stalks , cut into 2cm / 1" pieces
- 2 bay leaves
- 3 sprigs thyme (or sub with 1 tsp dried thyme leaves)

Directions:

1. Cut the beef into 5cm/2" chunks. Pat dry then sprinkle with salt and pepper.

2. Heat oil in a heavy based pot over high heat. Add beef in batches and brown well all over. Remove onto plate. Repeat with remaining beef.

3. Lower heat to medium. If the pot is looking dry, add oil.

4. Cook garlic and onion for 3 minutes until softening, then add bacon.

5. Cook until bacon is browned, then stir through carrot and celery.

6. Add flour, and stir for 1 minute to cook off the flour.

7. Add Guinness, chicken broth/stock and tomato paste. Mix well (to ensure flour dissolves well), add bay leaves and thyme.

8. Return beef into the pot (including any juices). Liquid level should just cover - see video or photos.

9. Cover, lower heat so it is bubbling gently. Cook for 2 hours - the beef should be pretty tender by now. Remove lid then simmer for a further 30 - 45 minutes or until the beef falls apart at a touch, the sauce has reduced and thickened slightly.

10. Skim off fat on surface, if desired. Adjust salt and pepper to taste. Remove bay leaves and thyme.

11. Serve with creamy mashed potatoes!!

NOTES

Guinness Beer is a dark coloured rich Irish beer and it is the key flavouring for the sauce of this stew. You CANNOT taste it in the finished dish, it just melds into an amazing sauce. In Australia you can get Guinness at all major liquor stores.

There is no non alcoholic substitute unfortunately. If you cannot consume alcohol, substitute the Guinness with 2 cups water + 1 tbsp Worcestershire sauce + 2 beef bouillon cubes crumbled. This will make it a classic beef stew. Taste FAB, it just isn't Irish Guinness Stew!

Other cooking methods:

- OVEN: Cover and bake for 2 1/2 hours at 160C / 320F. Remove then cook for a further 30 - 45 minutes to reduce sauce, per recipe.- SLOW COOKER: Reduce chicken broth by 1 cup. After you add the Guinness and broth/stock into the pot, bring to simmer and ensure you scrape the bottom of the pot well. Transfer everything into slow cooker. Add remaining ingredients per recipe. Cook on low for 8 hours. If sauce needs more thickening, simmer with slow cooker lid off (if you have that function), to ladle some of the sauce into a separate saucepan and reduce on stove.- PRESSURE COOKER: Follow slow cooker instructions, cook on HIGH for 40 minutes (this might seem longer than most but we're using chuck here which needs to be cooked for a long time until tender and also the pieces are large).

FLOUR: I prefer my stew sauce a bit thick, not watery, so I always add flour to slightly thicken the sauce. Some recipes say to dust beef with flour before browning - I prefer not to use this method because the flour burns then this permeates throughout the whole stew.

Beef vs Chicken Broth - I use chicken broth because the flavour is slightly more mild which lets the guinness flavour come through more. But beef broth works just as well and you can definitely still taste the Guinness!!

Slow Cooker Beer Stew

Servings: 4
Cooking Time: 5 Hours

Ingredients:

- 1 kg chuck beef steak, diced
- 1 tbs plain flour
- 2 washed potatoes, cut in half then thinly sliced
- 1 large onion sliced
- 1 large carrot thinly sliced
- 1 tsp cracked black pepper
- 1 tbs Massel* Beef Stock powder
- 375ml beer
- 2 tbsp soy sauce
- 2 bay leaves
- 1 tbsp cornflour
- 1 tbsp gravy powder
- 2 tbsp water

Directions:

1. Place beef and flour in a large bag and shake to coat beef in the flour. Add this floured beef to slow cooker.

2. Add potato, carrot and onion. Sprinkle over stock powder and pepper. Pour over beef and soy sauce and stir to combine then place bay leaves on top.

3. Slow cook on high for 5hrs or low for 8hrs.

4. Combine cornflour, gravy powder and water to make thin paste and stir through beer stew in the last 15mins of cooking to thicken gravy prior to serving.

5. Serve with sweet potato mash and steamed broccolini.

Slow-cooker Chicken Tortilla Soup

Servings: 8
Cooking Time: 3 Hours

Ingredients:

- 1 pound shredded, cooked chicken
- 1 (15 ounce) can whole peeled tomatoes, mashed
- 1 (10 ounce) can enchilada sauce
- 1 (4 ounce) can chopped green chile peppers
- 1 medium onion, chopped
- 2 cloves garlic, minced
- 2 cups water
- 1 (14.5 ounce) can chicken broth
- 1 teaspoon cumin
- 1 teaspoon chili powder
- 1 teaspoon salt
- ¼ teaspoon black pepper
- 1 bay leaf
- 1 (10 ounce) package frozen corn
- 1 tablespoon chopped cilantro
- 7 corn tortillas
- 2 tablespoons vegetable oil, or as needed

Directions:

1. Place chicken, tomatoes, enchilada sauce, green chiles, onion, and garlic into a slow cooker. Pour in water and chicken broth; season with cumin, chili

powder, salt, pepper, and bay leaf. Stir in corn and cilantro. Cover and cook on Low for 6 to 8 hours or on High for 3 to 4 hours.

2. When the soup is almost finished, preheat the oven to 400 degrees F (200 degrees C).

3. Lightly brush both sides of tortillas with oil. Cut tortillas into strips, then spread on a baking sheet.

4. Bake in the preheated oven until crisp, 10 to 15 minutes. Sprinkle tortilla strips over soup before serving.

Slow Cooker Creamy Tortellini Soup

Servings: 10
Cooking Time: 4 Hours

Ingredients:

- 1 pound (500 g) ground Italian sausage (or ground chicken, turkey or beef), browned*
- 1 onion, chopped
- 2 large carrots, chopped
- 2 stalks celery, chopped
- 4 cloves garlic, minced
- 1 tablespoon Italian seasoning
- 2 teaspoon beef bouillon powder (or chicken)
- 1/2 teaspoon salt
- 4 cups beef broth (or chicken or vegetable broth -- I use low sodium)
- 1/4 cup cornstarch mixed and dissolved in 1/4 cup water
- 36 ounces evaporated milk or half and half
- 12 ounce packet three cheese tortellini (I used dried not fresh; choose any flavour you like)
- 5 cups fresh baby spinach
- 1 cup milk

Directions:

1. Place the browned sausage, onion, carrots, celery, garlic, Italian seasoning, beef bouillon powder, salt, and broth in a 6-quart / litre slow cooker bowl. Cover and cook on high for 4 hours or low for 7 hours.

2. Uncover and skim any fat that is sitting on the top of the soup with a spoon; discard. Stir in the cornstarch mixture with the evaporated milk (or half and half or cream). Add the tortellini and mix well. Cover again and cook on HIGH heat setting for a further 45 minutes until the soup has thickened, and the tortellini is soft and cooked through.

3. Add in the spinach, pressing the leaves down to completely submerse into the liquid. Cover again for a further 5-10 minutes until the leaves have wilted.

4. Pour in milk in 1/3 cup increments, as needed, to reach your desired thickness and consistency (I needed 1 cup); taste test and season with extra salt ONLY if needed, and pepper to suit your tastes.

5. Serve with crusty warmed bread

NOTES

*Italian sausage gives this soup an amazing flavour, but you can substitute it with ground chicken, turkey or beef sausage. OR use plain ground meats if you don't like sausage. For vegetarian options, leave the meat out all together.

The soup thickens as it cools and absorbs quite a lot of liquid. Extra milk may be needed when reheating leftovers to reach your desired level of creaminess.

Vegetable Beef Soup

Servings: 5
Cooking Time: 1 Hours 50 Minutes

Ingredients:

- 1.5 tbsp olive oil , separated
- 500g/1 lb stewing beef , cut into 1.75cm / 2/3" cubes
- 1/2 tsp salt and pepper
- 1 onion , chopped
- 3 garlic , minced
- 2 celery , cut into 0.8 cm / 1/3" slices
- 3 carrots , cut into 0.5 cm / 1/5" thick slices (halve larger ones)
- 4 tbsp flour
- 2 1/2 cups (625ml) beef broth/stock , low sodium
- 1 1/2 cups (375ml) dry red wine, Guinness beer or stout
- 1.5 cups (375ml) water
- 2 tbsp tomato paste
- 2 bay leaves
- 1 tsp thyme dried
- 1 cup frozen peas
- 2 potatoes (any), cut into 1.5cm / 2/3" cubes
- Buttery mushrooms (optional):
- 1 tbsp (15g) butter or oil
- 200g/ 6oz small mushrooms , quartered or halved

Directions:

1. Heat 1 tbsp oil until very hot in a large, heavy based pot over high heat.

2. Pat beef dry with paper towels, then sprinkle with salt and pepper.

3. Brown beef aggressively in 2 or 3 batches, adding more oil if needed. Remove browned beef into a bowl.

4. If pot looks dry, add a touch more oil.

5. Add garlic and onion, cook for 2 minutes.

6. Add carrot and celery, cook for 2 minutes or until onion is translucent.

7. Stir in flour, then slowly pour in beef broth while constantly stirring.

8. Add beer, water, tomato paste, bay leaves and thyme, stir well. Then add the beef back in.

9. Cover, adjust heat to medium low so it's bubbling gently. Simmer 1 hr 15 min or until beef is pretty tender.

10. Add potatoes and peas, simmer for a further 20 minutes without the lid. Add cooked mushrooms in the last 5 minutes.

11. The soup is ready when the potatoes are cooked and beef is very tender

12. Adjust salt and pepper to taste (I like lots of pepper in this!).

13. Ladle into bowls. Sprinkle with parsley and serve with crusty bread if desired. Try quick Cheesy Garlic Bread or super easy Irish Soda Bread!

14. Buttery Mushrooms (optional):

15. Melt butter in a large skillet over medium high heat. Add mushrooms and cook for 5 minutes until browned. Sprinkle with salt and pepper.

NOTES

Beef - Use any stewing or braising beef, usually sold pre cut into small pieces ideal for this recipe. Otherwise, get a slow cooking cut like chuck or boneless short rib, then cut the beef into pieces. Look for beef that's nicely marbled with fat for best results!

Red Wine, Guinness or Stout - will add incredible extra flavour into this soup broth! I use all 3, and enjoy them all. If you love Irish Beef Guinness Stew, you'll know what the Guinness does to add flavour.

Red wine - any dry, full bodied red wine. Cab Sauv and Merlots are ideal.

Guinness Beer and Stout are dark beers, labelled as such on the cans. You should find these at most liquor stores. Use some, drink some - or tip the whole can in an simmer for longer with the lid off!

Non alcoholic sub - add 400g/14 oz can of crushed tomato, 2 tsp Worcestershire sauce. This will add alternative flavour to compensate.

Storage - Like stew, it's even better the next day! Will keep for 4 to 5 days in the fridge. Also freezes perfectly.

Slow Cooker Spiced Parsnip Soup

Servings: 6
Cooking Time: 8 Hours

Ingredients:

- 750g parsnips, peeled and chopped
- 400g carrots, chopped
- 1 onion, chopped
- 2 large garlic cloves, crushed or finely grated
- 1-2 tbsp curry powder
- 1l vegetable stock

Directions:

1. Tip the parsnips, carrots, onions, garlic and curry powder into a slow cooker, and mix well so all the vegetables are coated in the curry powder. Pour in the vegetable stock, then mix again and season well.

2. Cook on low for 8 hrs. Transfer to a blender and blitz until smooth. If you prefer your soup a little looser, you can stir in a few splashes of boiled water from the kettle. Divide between bowls and season with ground black pepper before serving. Once completely cool, the soup will keep frozen up to three months. Defrost completely in the fridge overnight, then reheat in a pan until piping hot before serving.

Mexican Chicken Stew

Servings: 4
Cooking Time: 25 Minutes

Ingredients:

- 1 tbsp vegetable oil
- 1 medium onion, finely chopped
- 3 garlic cloves, finely chopped
- ½ tsp dark brown sugar
- 1 tsp chipotle paste
- 400g can chopped tomatoes
- 4 skinless, boneless chicken breasts
- 1 small red onion, sliced into rings
- a few coriander leaves
- corn tortillas, or rice to serve

Directions:

1. Heat the oil in a medium saucepan. Add the onion and cook for 5 mins or until softened and starting to turn golden, adding the garlic for the final min. Stir in the sugar, chipotle paste and tomatoes. Put the chicken into the pan, spoon over the sauce, and simmer gently for 20 mins until the chicken has cooked (add a splash of water if the sauce gets too dry).

2. Remove the chicken from the pan and shred with 2 forks, then stir back into the sauce. Scatter with a little red onion, the coriander, and serve with remaining red onion, tortillas or rice.

3. If you want to use a slow cooker, cook the onion and garlic as above, then put into your slow cooker with the sugar, chipotle, tomatoes and chicken.

Cover and cook on High for 2 hours. Remove the chicken and shred then serve as above.

4. RECIPE TIPS
5. CHIPOTLE PASTE
6. Chipotle chillies - smoked Mexican jalapeño chillies - add an authentic smoky flavour to this stew. Chipotle paste is usually easier to find than the dried chillies.

Slow-cooker Chicken Tortilla Soup

Servings: 6

Ingredients:

- 1 lb. boneless skinless chicken breasts
- 1 (15-oz.) can black beans, rinsed
- 1 c. frozen corn
- 2 bell peppers, chopped
- 1 white onion, chopped
- 1 (15-oz.) can fire-roasted tomatoes
- 1/4 c. freshly chopped cilantro, plus more for garnish
- 3 cloves garlic, minced
- 1 tbsp. ground cumin
- 1 tbsp. chili powder
- 1 tsp. kosher salt
- 2 c. low-sodium chicken broth
- 1 c. shredded Monterey jack
- 1 tbsp. extra-virgin olive oil
- 3 small corn tortillas, cut into strips
- Sliced avocado, for serving
- Sour cream, for serving
- Lime wedges, for serving

Directions:

1. In a large slow cooker, combine chicken, black beans, corn, peppers, onion, fire-roasted tomatoes, cilantro, garlic, cumin, chili powder, salt, and chicken broth.
2. Cover and cook on low until chicken is cooked and falling apart, 5 to 6 hours.

3. Shred chicken with a fork, then top soup with Monterey Jack and cover to let melt, 5 minutes more.
4. Meanwhile, make tortilla crisps: In a large skillet over medium heat, heat oil. Add tortilla strips and cook until crispy and golden, 3 minutes. Transfer to a paper towel-lined plate and season with salt.
5. Serve soup topped with tortilla crisps, avocado, sour cream, cilantro, and lime.

Slow Cooker Beef Stew

Servings: 6
Cooking Time: 4 Hours

Ingredients:

- 2 pounds beef stew meat, cut into 1-inch pieces
- ¼ cup all-purpose flour
- ½ teaspoon salt
- ½ teaspoon ground black pepper
- 1 ½ cups beef broth
- 4 medium carrots, sliced
- 3 medium potatoes, diced
- 1 medium onion, chopped
- 1 stalk celery, chopped
- 1 teaspoon Worcestershire sauce
- 1 teaspoon ground paprika
- 1 clove garlic, minced
- 1 large bay leaf

Directions:

1. Gather ingredients.
2. Place meat in slow cooker.
3. Mix flour, salt, and pepper together in a small bowl. Pour over meat, and stir until meat is coated.
4. Add beef broth, carrots, potatoes, onion, celery, Worcestershire sauce, paprika, garlic, and bay leave; stir to combine.
5. Cover, and cook until beef is tender enough to cut with a spoon, on Low for 8 to 12 hours, or on High for 4 to 6 hours.
6. Serve hot and enjoy!

NOTES:

This original recipe submission called for slow cooking on Low for 10 to 12 hours. When making for this recipe, our food stylists found a cook time of 8 hours on Low (or 4 hours on High) was sufficient. Please stir and check doneness along the way to be sure your meat is cooked properly.

Slow Cooker Chicken Pot Pie Soup

Servings: 6
Cooking Time: 8 Hours

Ingredients:

- 1 1/2 cups carrots sliced
- 1 1/2 cups celery sliced
- 1 cup white onion diced
- 1 tsp. dried basil
- 1/2 tsp. dried leaf thyme
- 1/2 tsp. salt
- 1/4 tsp. pepper
- 1 bay leaf
- 1 1/2 lbs boneless skinless chicken breasts
- 32 oz. broth
- Add at the end
- 1 cup frozen peas
- 1 cup heavy cream
- For Serving
- 10 oz. puff pastry shells

Directions:

1. Cooking Instructions:
2. Place the carrots, celery, onion, basil, thyme, salt, pepper, bay leaf, chicken and chicken broth in to the slow cooker, stir.
3. Cover and cook on LOW for 8 hours.
4. After the cooking time is done add the peas, and heavy cream. Stir and discard the bay leaf.
5. Cook the puff pastry shells according to package directions.
6. Serve the soup topped with the puff pastries.
7. To make this into a freezer meal:

8. Place everything but the peas and heavy cream into a freezer gallon ziplock bag.
9. Squeeze out all the air, seal, and freeze for up to one month.
10. Mark on the bag that one cup of peas and one cup of heavy cream needs to be added at the end of the cooking time. Write the cooking setting and length as well (Low for 8 hours).
11. To make after being frozen:
12. Place the frozen bag of soup in the fridge for 24 hours to thaw. Dump the contents of the bag in to the slow cooker. Cook as directed above.

Pancetta And Borlotti Bean Soup With Toasts

Servings: 4
Cooking Time: 7 Hours 10 Minutes

Ingredients:

- 190g (1 cup) dried borlotti beans
- 1 tsp extra virgin olive oil
- 1 large brown onion, finely chopped
- 4 celery sticks, finely chopped
- 1 large carrot, peeled, finely chopped
- 75g pancetta, finely chopped
- 3 garlic cloves, crushed
- 2 tsp fresh rosemary, finely chopped
- 1 long fresh red chilli, deseeded, finely chopped
- 500ml (2 cups) Massel chicken style liquid stock or vegetable liquid stock
- 500ml (2 cups) water
- 100g trimmed cavolo nero (Tuscan cabbage), chopped
- 4 slices rye bread, grilled
- 1 1/2 tbsp fresh basil pesto
- Baby herbs, to serve

Directions:

1. Place beans in a bowl. Cover with cold water. Set aside for 8 hours or overnight to soak. Drain. Place in a saucepan. Cover with cold water. Bring to the

boil over mediumhigh heat. Cook for 10 minutes. Drain well.

2. Heat the oil in a non-stick frying pan over medium heat. Cook the onion, celery, carrot and pancetta, stirring, for 5 minutes or until soft. Add the garlic, rosemary and chilli. Cook, stirring, for 1 minute or until aromatic.

3. Place the onion mixture, beans, stock and water in a large (6L) slow cooker. Cover. Cook on low for 6-7 hours. Stir through the cavolo nero and season with black pepper.

4. Spread bread with pesto. Divide soup among bowls. Top with herbs. Serve with toast.

NOTES

A valuable source of low-GI carbohydrate, borlotti beans provide long lasting energy and are an excellent source of protien and dietary fibre. Slow cookers are perfect for cooking dried legumes because they take a long time to cook.

Authentic Irish Stew Recipe

Servings: 4
Cooking Time: 2 Hours

Ingredients:

- 800g lamb cutlets bone removed
- 2 tbsp vegetable oil
- 500g potatoes, peeled and cut into chunks
- 2 onions
- 150g carrots, chopped
- 2 leeks, sliced
- 100g pearl barley
- 750ml lamb stock
- ¼ of cabbage, sliced
- 20g spring onions, sliced
- 10g parsley, roughly chopped

Directions:

1. Preheat the oven to 160'C. Heat half the oil in a large frying pan over a medium heat. Add the lamb cutlets and fry for 3-5 mins on each side until brown.

2. Transfer the lamb to a large casserole dish with a lid. Add the potatoes, onions, leeks, carrots and pearl barley. Add the stock, season and cover. Cook in the oven for 1hr.

3. Add the cabbage to the dish and return to the oven for 1hr, adding a splash more stock if beginning to look dry. Scatter with spring onions and parsley to serve.

Slow Cooker Spiced Chicken And Chickpea Soup

Servings: 4

Ingredients:

- 1 tbsp olive oil
- 2 Coles RSPCA Approved Australian Chicken Breast Fillets
- 1 red onion, finely chopped
- 1 carrot, peeled, finely chopped
- 2 celery sticks, finely chopped
- 1 tbsp Moroccan seasoning
- 400g can diced tomatoes
- 4 cups (1L) chicken stock
- 1/2 cup (100g) green lentils
- 1/4 cup (50g) red lentils
- 400g can chickpeas, rinsed, drained
- 1 cup (150g) frozen broad beans, thawed, peeled
- Greek-style yoghurt, to serve
- Coriander leaves, to serve
- Mint leaves, to serve

Directions:

1. Heat the oil in a large frying pan over high heat. Cook the chicken for 2 mins each side or until brown all over.

2. Transfer the chicken to a slow cooker. Add the onion, carrot, celery, Moroccan seasoning, tomato, stock, combined lentils and chickpeas. Cover and cook for 4 hours on high (or 6 hours on low) or until the chicken is very tender.

3. Use tongs to transfer the chicken to a plate. Coarsely shred and return to the soup with the broad beans. Season.

4. Ladle soup among serving bowls. Serve with yoghurt, coriander and mint.

Slow Cooker Chicken Enchilada Soup

Servings: 5
Cooking Time: 8 Hours

Ingredients:

- 1 cup diced white onion
- 1 TBSP. minced jalapeno more if you can handle extreme heat
- ⅓ cup chopped cilantro
- 8.75 oz. can corn, drained
- 10 oz. can red enchilada sauce
- 10.75 oz. can cream of chicken soup
- 1.5 lbs. boneless skinless chicken breasts
- 32 oz. box chicken broth
- Serving Suggestions
- Shredded Cheese cheddar or Monterey Jack
- Tortilla Chips

Directions:

1. Cooking Instructions: (follow freezer meal instructions before cooking if you want to freeze)

2. Place everything into a 6-quart slow cooker and stir. Cover and cook on Low for 8 hours without opening the lid during the cooking time.

3. Freezer Meal Preparations: (this recipe makes 1 freezer bag):

4. Write the name of the meal, date and cooking time on the very bottom edge of the a gallon size Ziplock bag. Place the ziplock bag into a tall large container, fold down the lip of the bag so the zip part won't get food all over it. Add the ingredients into to the bag in the order shown. Pull the bag out of the container and squeeze all the air out before sealing. Place flat in the freezer. Freeze for no longer than a month for best results.

5. To prepare after being frozen:

6. Place the freezer bag in the fridge to thaw 24-48 hours before you are ready to cook.

7. Cook according to directions above.

Slow-cooker Spiced Split-pea Soup With Harissa Labneh

Servings: 4
Cooking Time: 8 Hours 10 Minutes

Ingredients:

- 2 tbsp extra virgin olive oil
- 1 large brown onion, finely chopped
- 2 celery sticks, thinly sliced
- 2 carrots, peeled, cut into 1cm pieces
- 1 red capsicum, deseeded, cut into 1cm pieces
- 1 tbsp fresh coriander stem, finely chopped
- 1 1/2 tbsp Moroccan seasoning
- 1/2 tsp ground cinnamon
- 1L (4 cups) Massel salt reduced chicken style liquid stock
- 650g smoked ham hock
- 400g can diced tomatoes
- 210g (1 cup) dried yellow split peas
- Fresh coriander leaves, to serve
- Toasted Lebanese bread, to serve
- Lemon wedges, to serve
- Harissa labneh
- 520g (2 cups) Greek-style yoghurt
- 1 tsp sea salt
- 1 tbsp harissa
- 1 tbsp extra virgin olive oil
- Method
- For the harissa labneh, place a sieve over a large bowl. Line the sieve with a double layer of muslin. Combine the yoghurt and salt in a bowl. Place the yoghurt mixture in the centre of the muslin. Bring the edges together to enclose. Twist to secure and tie with kitchen string. Place in the fridge for 6-8 hours or overnight to drain.
- Meanwhile, heat oil in a large frying pan over medium heat. Add onion, celery, carrot and

capsicum. Cook, stirring, for 4-5 minutes or until softened. Add coriander stem, seasoning and cinnamon. Stir for 2 minutes or until aromatic. Transfer to a 5.5L slow cooker.

- Add stock, ham hock, tomato and split peas to slow cooker. Season with pepper. Stir to combine. Cover and cook on Low for 6-8 hours or until ham is very tender and falls away from the bone.
- Remove the ham hock from the slow cooker. Use 2 forks to remove the meat from the bone. Discard the bone and rind. Shred the meat and return to the soup.
- Remove labneh from muslin and place on a plate. Combine harissa and oil in a bowl. Spoon over the labneh. Ladle the soup into serving bowls. Top with coriander and serve with the bread, harissa labneh and lemon wedges.

Slow Cooker Mexican Chicken Soup

Servings: 8
Cooking Time: 9 Hours 45 Minutes

Ingredients:

- 1 1/4 cup dried pinto beans soaked overnight
- 1 1/2 lbs. chicken boneless skinless chicken breasts
- 1 small white onion diced
- 7 oz. can fire roasted diced chiles
- 10 oz. can red enchilada sauce
- 14.5 oz. can Mexican style stewed tomatoes
- 32 oz. box chicken broth
- 1/4 tsp. pepper
- 1/4 tsp. garlic powder
- 1/2 tsp. dried oregano
- 1/2 tsp. cumin
- 1 cup dry brown Minute Rice

Directions:

1. The beans need to be soaked over night in water to help soften them up. Do this by adding the beans to a medium sized bowl and covering with water.
2. Add the soaked beans, chicken, chiles, enchilada sauce, stewed tomatoes, chicken broth, pepper,

garlic powder, oregano, and cumin to the slow cooker. Stir. DO NOT ADD MINUTE RICE YET.
3. Cover and cook on LOW for 9 hours without opening the lid during the cooking time.
4. Shred the chicken with 2 forks.
5. Add the dried brown Minute rice to the slow cooker, stir.
6. Cover and let cook on low for 45 minutes more.

NOTES

I only use Minute rice (instant) in the slow cooker. Regular rice tends to get gummy in the slow cooker.

Slow Cooker Irish Lamb Chop Stew

Ingredients:

- 8 forequarter lamb chops
- 4 bacon rashers, cut into strips
- 1 tbsp plain flour
- 6 baby potatoes, thinly sliced
- 3 carrots, thinly sliced
- 1 brown onion cut into wedges
- 1 leek small, thinly sliced
- 150g cabbage, thinly sliced
- 250ml Beef Style Liquid Stock
- 2 tbs fresh flat-leaf parsley finely chopped

Directions:

1. Add the potato slices, carrot slices, onion wedges and leek slices to slow cooker, toss gently to mix.
2. Place lamb chops and flour in a bag and toss to coat. Lay floured chops on top of vegetables in the slow cooker.
3. Add the bacon and stock and finish with the shredded cabbage on top.
4. Slow cook on HIGH for 6 hours.
5. Season well and sprinkle with parsley and serve.

NOTES

For hard root vegetables, like carrot, potato etc it's best to keep them thin sliced to make sure they cook lovely and tender by the end of cooking time in the slow cooker.

Slow cooking needs less liquids than other cooking methods. The closed lid means less evaporation, and the liquids released from the meat and condensation from the lid during cooking all adds to extra liquids by the end.

For this reason, minimal liquids are added at the start, but don't worry you'll have plenty by the end.

Herby Bean Sausage Stew

Servings: 4

Ingredients:

- 8 chipolatas
- 2 x 420g/15oz can mixed beans
- 2 x 400g/14oz cans chopped tomato
- 1 tsp dried basil
- 2 tsp dried oregano
- 1 tbsp sugar

Directions:

1. Heat a large non-stick frying pan, then brown the sausages for 3-5 mins over a high heat. Drain the beans, then add to the pan with the chopped tomatoes, herbs and sugar. Season well and bring to the boil. Simmer for 10 mins until the sausages are cooked through and the sauce has thickened, coating the beans.
2. RECIPE TIPS
3. ADDING SUGAR
4. Adding a little sugar to a tomato-based sauce brings out the natural sweetness of the tomatoes. It's also a great way to perk up under-ripe fresh tomatoes.
5. IF YOU WANT TO USE A SLOW COOKER
6. Brown your sausages in a non-stick frying pan over a high heat for 3-5 minutes. Transfer them to the slow cooker pot with the beans. Add one can of tomatoes, then just the chopped tomatoes from the other can- sieve away the juice. Stir in your herbs and sugar with some seasoning, then cover and cook on Low overnight or for up to 8 hours.

Creamy Chicken & Broccoli Stew

Servings: 8
Cooking Time: 6 Hours

Ingredients:

- 8 bone-in chicken thighs, skinned (about 3 pounds)
- 1 cup Italian salad dressing
- 1/2 cup white wine or chicken broth
- 6 tablespoons butter, melted, divided
- 1 tablespoon dried minced onion
- 1 tablespoon garlic powder
- 1 tablespoon Italian seasoning
- 3/4 teaspoon salt, divided
- 3/4 teaspoon pepper, divided
- 1 can (10-3/4 ounces) condensed cream of mushroom soup, undiluted
- 1 package (8 ounces) cream cheese, softened
- 2 cups frozen broccoli florets, thawed
- 2 pounds red potatoes, quartered

Directions:

1. Place chicken in a 4-qt. slow cooker. Combine the salad dressing, wine, 4 tablespoons butter, onion, garlic powder, Italian seasoning, 1/2 teaspoon salt and 1/2 teaspoon pepper in a small bowl; pour over chicken.
2. Cover and cook on low for 5 hours. Skim off fat. Remove chicken from slow cooker with a slotted spoon; shred chicken with 2 forks and return to slow cooker. Combine the soup, cream cheese and 2 cups of liquid from slow cooker in a small bowl until blended; add to slow cooker. Cover and cook 45 minutes longer or until chicken is tender, adding the broccoli during the last 30 minutes of cooking.
3. Meanwhile, place potatoes in a large saucepan and cover with water. Bring to a boil. Reduce heat; cover and simmer until tender, 15-20 minutes. Drain and return to pan. Mash potatoes with the remaining 2 tablespoons butter and 1/4 teaspoon each salt and pepper.
4. Serve chicken and broccoli mixture with potatoes.

Slow-cooked Beef And Barley Soup

Servings: 4
Cooking Time: 8 Hours

Ingredients:

- 2 tsp olive oil
- 500g beef blade steak, trimmed, chopped
- 2 carrots, peeled, finely chopped
- 2 celery sticks, trimmed, chopped
- 1 large brown onion, finely chopped
- 2 garlic cloves, crushed
- 2 tsp fresh thyme leaves
- 500ml (2 cups) Massel beef style liquid stock
- 375ml (1 1/2 cups) water
- 400g can diced tomatoes
- 75g (1/3 cup) pearl barley, rinsed, drained
- 100g trimmed Tuscan cabbage, shredded
- Chopped fresh continental parsley, to serve
- Baby parsley sprigs, to serve

Directions:

1. Heat half the oil in a saucepan over high heat. Add beef. Cook, stirring, for 2-3 minutes or until well browned. Place in slow cooker.
2. Heat the remaining oil in the saucepan over medium heat. Add the carrot, celery and onion. Cook, stirring, for 5-6 minutes or until soft. Add the garlic and thyme. Cook, stirring, for 1 minute or until aromatic. Return the beef to the pan. Add stock, water and tomatoes. Bring to the boil. Add to slow cooker. Cover and cook on low for 6 hours. Add the barley and Tuscan cabbage and cook for 2 hours or until barley is cooked and cabbage is wilted.
3. Season to taste with freshly ground pepper. Sprinkle with the parsley.

Slow Cooker Curried Mince And Potato Stew Recipe

Servings: 6
Cooking Time: 5 Hours

Ingredients:

- 2 large potatoes, cut small into 1cm cubes
- 3 cups shredded green cabbage
- 700g beef mince
- 1 large onion, finely chopped
- 4 tsp minced garlic
- 2 tsp curry powder
- 1 tbsp chicken stock powder
- 2 tbsp tomato paste

Directions:

1. Spray slow cooker bowl with oil. Add potato to slow cooker and top with cabbage.
2. Combine all the remaining ingredients and ½ cup warm water in a large bowl. Place meat mixture on top of the cabbage (don't stir). We want to potatoes to stay down the bottom of the slow cooker for the first several hours so don't mix it all together at this point. The meat mixture stays on top of the vegetables.
3. Cook on low for 3 hours. Stir to combine ingredients and then cook for a further 2 hours.
4. Serve with a fresh side salad or crusty bread.

NOTES

It's important to keep these potato cubes small to ensure they are tender by the end of cooking. Another alternative you could do instead if you want larger chunks is to par boil them first to slightly soften before adding.

We used 2 tsp mild curry powder with younger children in the house who don't like anything "too spicy!" If you like more heat you could double this to 1 tbsp or to your personal preference.

SNACKS AND APPETIZERS RECIPES

Slow Cooker Creamy Ranch Dip

Servings: 10
Cooking Time: 2 Hours

Ingredients:

- 16 oz can refried beans
- 15.5 oz. can pinto beans, drained
- 16 oz. sour cream
- 3 cups shredded sharp cheddar cheese, divided
- 1 oz. packet ranch dressing mix
- For Serving
- 2 cups salsa

Directions:

1. Add the refried beans, pinto beans, sour cream, 1 cup of the cheese, and the ranch dressing packet to the slow cooker. Stir and flatten out. Clean up the edges with a paper towel for a cleaner look.
2. Sprinkle over the remaining cheese.
3. Cover and cook on HIGH for 2 to 2 1/2 hours or until hot and bubbly. Serve with salsa and chips.

Slow Cooker Bacon Wrapped Little Smokies

Servings: 8

Ingredients:

- 1 ½ cups brown sugar divided
- 16 oz. bacon (you will have some leftover)
- 14 oz. little smokies Find these by the bacon or packaged lunch meat at the store.
- ¼ cup pineapple juice
- toothpicks don't forget to buy these!

Directions:

1. On a cutting board, cut the slices of bacon into thirds. Wrap each little smokie with bacon and secure with a toothpick. Set aside.
2. To your slow cooker add HALF of the brown sugar (¾ cup). Place the bacon wrapped little smokies on top of that brown sugar.

3. Sprinkle over the remaining ¾ cup brown sugar. Drizzle over the pineapple juice.
4. (NOTE THE COOK TIME IS 4 HOURS, BUT YOU WILL NEED TO ROTATE THE SMOKIES AT THE 3 HOUR MARK)
5. Place the lid on the slow cooker and set to high. At the 3 hour mark, you will notice that the ones in the middle will look less cooked than the outside ones. You are going to move the center little smokies to the outside edge and put those little smokies in the middle. I do this with a pair of tongs. Cook for 1 more hour on high.
6. Serve immediatley, or you can keep these on warm for 2 hours for your party. Do not drain the sauce.

NOTES

Want to cook in the oven? Place the little smokies in a glass 9x13 pan with the other ingredients. Bake uncovered for 30-45 minutes until the bacon is done.
Any leftover sausages can be placed in an airtight container and kept in the fridge for up to 4 days. Reheat them on a baking sheet, sheet pan, or cookie sheet lined with aluminum foil. Place them in a preheated oven and cook until warm.

Slow Cooker Corn Dip

Servings: 8
Cooking Time: 2 Hours

Ingredients:

- 4 cups frozen corn
- 8 oz. cream cheese softened
- 4 oz. pepper Jack cheese shredded
- 4 oz. Colby Jack cheese shredded
- ½ cup sour cream
- 1 Tbsp. hot sauce optional
- 2 green onions chopped
- 1 tsp. garlic powder
- 1 tsp. cumin
- ½ tsp. salt
- ½ tsp. pepper
- Optional Toppings

- cilantro
- paprika or Old Bay seasoning
- diced tomatoes
- jalapenos
- queso fresca
- hot sauces

Directions:

1. To your slow cooker add all the ingredients and mix thoroughly. Cook on HIGH for 2 Hours or LOW for 4 hours, or until the dip is hot and bubbling. Stir occasionally.
2. Add toppings if desired and serve with tortilla chips, enjoy!

NOTES

Store in the refrigerator for up to 3 days in an airtight container. Reheat in the microwave or oven at 375°F until hot and bubbling.

To make in the oven: Preheat the oven to 375°F, prepare a casserole dish with nonstick cooking spray, mix all ingredients in a large bowl, transfer to casserole dish, bake for 20-25 minutes or until hot and bubbling. Fresh or drained canned corn can be used in place of frozen corn.

Use any cheese or combination of cheeses that you love, cheddar, monetary jack, gouda, mozzarella, provolone.

Nutrition:

- al values do no include chips or toppings.

Slow Cooker Beer Cheese Dip Recipe

Servings: 8
Cooking Time: 1 Hours

Ingredients:

- 16 oz. cream cheese (two 8-oz. packages)
- 8 oz. FRESH FINELY shredded sharp cheddar cheese (8 oz. block, not preshredded bagged cheese)
- 1/2 cup beer (I use pilsner or a light beer)
- 1/2 cup milk
- 1 tsp. garlic powder
- 1 Tbsp. dijon mustard
- 2 tsp. Worcestershire sauce

- 1/2 tsp. cayenne (or paprika if you don't want any spice)
- For serving
- pretzel bites, pita chips, kielbasa, or tortilla chips

Directions:

1. Cube the cream cheese and add to the slow cooker. Add the sharp cheddar cheese, beer, milk, dijon mustard and seasonings.
2. Stir.
3. Place the lid on the slow cooker and cook on HIGH For 1 hour or until smooth, melty and hot. (stirring occasionally).

NOTES

Not sure what kind of beer to use? Pilsner or your favorite beer is the best. Don't use something you wouldn't drink. If you don't drink beer, but love beer cheese, use a very light beer such as bud light.

Alcohol does not completely cook off in the slow cooker. Keep that in mind when serving anyone who doesn't drink alcohol, including kids.

Add any leftovers to an airtight container and store in the fridge for a couple of days. In most cases, the dip may thicken so when reheating it, you may want to add a bit more milk to help make it creamy again.

Slow Cooker Salsa

Servings: 15
Cooking Time: 3 Hours

Ingredients:

- 6-7 fresh Roma tomatoes about 1 pound no need to chop, or core, leave whole
- 30 oz. fire roasted tomatoes (two 15-oz. cans)
- 1 white onion peeled cut into 8 wedges
- 3 jalapeños tops cut off
- 4 whole garlic cloves peeled
- Wait to add these items
- 1 bunch cilantro
- 1 lime
- 1 ¼ tsp. salt put in slowly, test it to taste
- 1 bunch green onions sliced (don't blend up, just stir these in)

Directions:

1. Put the Roma tomatoes, fire roasted tomatoes, onion, jalapeños and garlic in the slow cooker.
2. Cook on high for 3 hours, the tomatoes will look like they exploded, and the vegetables will be mostly soft.
3. In 2 batches (or one if it fits) scoop the items and juices from the slow cooker into your blender or food processor, and add the cilantro (tear off the big chunk stems and discard, some stems are ok).
4. Place the lid on. Pulse until salsa is the consistency you would like.
5. Pour into a large serving bowl or whatever container you want to store the salsa in. Add the salt to taste, juice of the lime, and the sliced green onion, stir.
6. Chill for at least 3 hours before serving. Serve with tortilla chips

NOTES

You do not have to use exact measurements for this recipe, make it your own! Love garlic or jalapenos? Add a few more. Just add the salt to taste carefully at the end.

This salsa should be poured into an airtight container and kept in the fridge for up to one week. Or you can freeze for up to two months. This recipe as is, is not safe for canning.

You can serve this salsa in more ways than just with chips! You can add it back to the slow cooker in recipes such as salsa chicken, Mexican beef or Velveeta dip.

Are you wondering why I don't add apple cider vinegar? I prefer no vinegar in fresh salsa; adding vinegar makes it tastes like store-bought jarred salsa.

This makes about 2 quarts, depending on the size of your vegetables.

Slow Cooker Meatballs And Little Smokies

Servings: 12
Cooking Time: 5 Hours

Ingredients:

- 28 oz. beef lil' smokies (two 14-oz. packages)
- 26 oz. frozen meatballs I use homestyle
- 20 oz. grape jelly I use Welch's squeeze bottle type

- 18 oz. Sweet Baby Ray's BBQ sauce original

Directions:

1. Add the meatballs and little smokies to the slow cooker.
2. Squeeze over the barbecue sauce and grape jelly.
3. Stir. Don't worry about mixing in the grape jelly completely, it will melt when it heats up.
4. Cook on LOW for 5 hours or HIGH for 3.5.
5. This may seem like a long cooking time, but these only improve with time. They will start absorbing the sauce later in the cooking time.

NOTES

Store any remaining meatballs and smokies in an airtight container. Keep them in the fridge for up to 4 days. Reheat them on the stovetop over medium heat.

For this appetizer, you can always use beef meatballs, pork meatballs, turkey meatballs, chicken meatballs, or a combination.

When it comes to flavor, you can play around with adding Heinz chili sauce, pineapple chunks, and chopped onion.

Slow Cooker Barbecue Meatballs

Servings: 10
Cooking Time: 2 Hours 30 Minutes

Ingredients:

- 40 oz. frozen meatballs (I use Safeway's Kitchen brand homestyle meatballs)
- 16 oz. Sweet Baby Ray's Original Barbecue Sauce
- 1 small sweet yellow onion diced

Directions:

1. Add the frozen meatballs to the slow cooker.
2. Add the diced white onion and barbecue sauce. Stir.
3. Cover and cook on high for 2.5 hours or on low for 4 hours. Stir occasionally so the meatballs won't burn on the edges.
4. Serve as an appetizer with toothpicks or as dinner on top of mashed potatoes or rice. Or you can serve on slider or hoagie rolls.
5. To keep warm at a party:

6. After the cooking time is up, set the slow cooker to the warm setting.
7. The meatballs can be kept warm for up to 3 hours. Check on the meatballs occasionally and stir. Add a splash of water if sauce seems to be dry.

NOTES

Use your favorite barbecue sauce in this reicpe and also you can use flavored barbecue sauces such as chipotle or spicy.

Warm Caramelised French Onion Slow Cooker Dip

Cooking Time: 1 Hours

Ingredients:

- 40g butter, chopped
- 3 large brown onions, halved, thinly sliced
- 2 tbsp water
- 2 shortcut bacon rashers, finely chopped
- 1 tbsp malt vinegar
- 2 tsp brown sugar
- 300g tub sour cream
- 250g spreadable cream cheese
- 1 tsp garlic powder
- 1 tsp Worcestershire sauce
- 1/4 cup light whole-egg mayonnaise
- 1 tbsp finely chopped fresh chives
- Assorted vegetables, to serve
- Crackers, to serve

Directions:

1. Melt butter in a medium frying pan over medium heat. Add onion. Cook, stirring occasionally for 15 minutes or until onion is golden brown. Add the water. Cook, stirring, until water is evaporated. Add bacon. Cook, stirring, for 2 minutes or until bacon is crisp. Add vinegar and sugar. Stir for 1 minute or until sugar has dissolved.
2. Set aside 1/4 of the onion mixture. Transfer remaining onion mixture to a slowcooker. Add sour cream, cream cheese, garlic powder and sauce. Stir to combine. Cover. Cook on HIGH for 45 minutes, stirring every 10 minutes or until mixture is smooth

and slightly thickened. Once thickened stir through the mayonnaise.
3. Transfer to a serving bowl. Top with reserved onion mixture and chives. Serve with vegetables and crackers.

Slow Cooker Grape Jelly Little Smokies Recipe

Servings: 15
Cooking Time: 2 Hours 30 Minutes

Ingredients:

- 28 oz. Lit'l Smokies two 14-oz. packages (I use pork and chicken)
- 18 oz. Concord grape jelly
- 12 oz. chili sauce

Directions:

1. Drain the little smokies and place them in a medium-sized bowl. Add the chili sauce and grape jelly and stir. Or you can add everything to the slow cooker instead and stir.
2. Place the lid on the slow cooker. Cook on HIGH For 5-3 hours or LOW for 4-5 hours, stirring occasionally.
3. Serve with toothpicks for guest to eat the smokies with and enjoy!

NOTES

Can I cook these on the stove-top?

If you don't have a crockpot, you can put everything in a pot and cook them over medium-low to medium heat. You'll need to stir it often to keep the sauce from sticking (and scorching). You can also cook these in the oven in a similar way.

How to store and reheat?

Place any leftovers in an airtight container and place them in the fridge. They will last for up to four days. If you opt-in for the freezer, ensure they are completely cooled, placed in a freezer-safe bag (or container), then stored. Freeze for up to three months. When you're ready to reheat them, let them thaw in the fridge first. Reheat on the stovetop or in the microwave.

Can I use hotdogs?

Yes! Hot dogs are a GREAT choice if you prefer. Slice the hot dogs into thirds, cutting them on an angle. Hot dogs soak up the sauce nicely and do not get soggy in the crockpot.

Variations

Barbecue Sauce - instead of chili sauce, replace it with BBQ sauce. These also come in a variety of flavors (spicy, tangy, honey, etc.). Add a teaspoon of Worcestershire sauce for more flavor.

Spicy - if you're looking to add some spice, consider adding sriracha, cayenne pepper, or some hot sauce. Or you can add one minced jalapeno to jazz up this recipe.

Cranberry sauce - add one can of jellied cranberry sauce along with chili sauce and brown sugar to create a flavorful homemade base.

Slow Cooker Taco Dip Recipe

Servings: 12
Cooking Time: 2 Hours

Ingredients:

- 1 lb. ground beef
- salt to taste
- pepper to taste
- onion powder to taste
- 16 oz. jar of Salsa I use mild pace picante
- 15 oz. jar nacho cheese found on chip aisle
- 16 oz. container sour cream
- 16 oz. can refried beans

Directions:

1. Brown meat in a skillet, add salt pepper, and onion powder. Drain and discard liquid.
2. Add meat to slow cooker.
3. Add salsa, nacho cheese, sour cream, refried beans to slow cooker.
4. Stir.
5. Cook on high for 2 hours, or until heated through.
6. Turn slow cooker to warm while serving.
7. Serve with tortilla chips

NOTES

Variations and Mixins

Taco Seasoning - Add taco seasoning to the ground beef instead of salt and pepper. Or you can make your own taco mix blend with chili powder, cumin, onion powder and garlic powder.

Cheddar cheese - Don't want to use nacho cheese? Use two cups of freshly shredded cheddar cheese or pepper jack cheese instead.

Cream cheese - For a more decadent dip, add softened cream cheese instead of sour cream. It will melt into the dip as it heats up.

Spicy - If everyone at your party loves spicy, chop 1-2 jalapenos and leave and don't remove the seeds. Or you can add two small cans of fire-roasted chiles.

How to serve

Serve as a dip with tortilla chips on the side

Serve as nachos! Pour the taco mixture over chips, and eat like nachos.

Top with your dip on your plate with a combination of shredded lettuce, shredded cheese, green peppers, green onions, diced tomatoes, and jalapeno slices. (Though this dip needs nothing extra, it's GREAT as it).

Slow Cooker Grape Jelly Meatballs

Servings: 15
Cooking Time: 4 Hours

Ingredients:

- 32 oz. bag frozen meatballs I use homestyle
- 20 oz. grape jelly I use Welch's
- 12 oz. Heinz chili sauce

Directions:

1. Put the frozen meatballs in the slow cooker. Add the grape jelly and chili sauce.
2. Stir until the meatballs are coated in the grape and chili sauce mixture.
3. Place the lid on the slow cooker.
4. Cook on HIGH for 2.5-3 hours or LOW for 4-5 hours. Stirring occasionally so the meatballs won't burn on the edges.
5. Keeping the grape jelly meatballs warm at a party:
6. Turn the slow cooker to warm. Can be kept warm at a party for 3+ hours. Stir often, and add a splash of water if the sauce thickens too much.

NOTES

What is chili sauce?

There are different types of chili sauce, the one in this recipe is near the ketchup in your grocery store (I use Heinz chili sauce).

Heinz chili sauce is made from tomatoes, garlic, sweet peppers, and aromatic spices

DO NOT use sriracha hot chili sauce or sweet Thai chili sauce unless you want it to be VERY spicy.

Can I use a different type of jam?

Yes, one of these jams or jellies can be used instead of grape jelly:

Strawberry jam or jelly

Apple jelly

Raspberry jam or preserves

What can I use instead of chili sauce?

Chili sauce works best in this recipe, if you can't make it to the store and are in a pinch you can use one of these options:

Ketchup - add a touch of onion, garlic and chili powder.

Barbecue sauce - any kind will work.

I can't find a 32-ounce bag of frozen meatballs?

This recipe is very flexible! You can use a slightly smaller bag or two bags that equal a little more than 32 ounces.

Will work fine, there is plenty of sauce in this recipe.

What to serve with grape jelly meatballs?

Serve as an appetizer with toothpicks at a party

With steamed rice

Over mashed potatoes

Can I use a different type of meatball?

Any style of frozen meatball can be used in this recipe such as Italian, Angus or even turkey.

If you are looking for a healthier meatball try Trader Joe's brand.

You can even use meatless meatballs !

Slow Cooker Queso Verde

Servings: 12
Cooking Time: 2 Hours 30 Minutes

Ingredients:

- 2 lbs. white Velveeta Cheese (I find this at Walmart)
- 1 cup milk
- 16 oz. jar salsa verde
- 16 oz. sour cream (can use cream cheese, but use a 1/2 cup more milk)
- 2 jalapenos minced

Directions:

1. Cut the Velveeta cheese into cubes. Add the velveeta and remaining ingredients to the slow cooker.
2. Cover and cook on HIGH for 5 hours, stirring occasionally.
3. Serve with chips and enjoy!

NOTES

Can I use a different kind of salsa?

If you can't find a green salsa, a red salsa with plenty of hatch chiles will work great. I find hatch salsa in the refrigerated section of the store.

How can I make this mild?

Use canned fire-roasted green chiles instead of jalapenos for a mild queso verde dip.

How to store?

This doesn't freeze well, but you can place it in the fridge for up to a week. You will need to add a touch of milk when reheating.

How to reheat:

The best way is on the stove in a small saucepan. Heat on medium heat and stir often. Add milk if it's too thick. Or you can heat a small amount at a time in the microwave until it's completely melted.

Slow Cooker Garlic Confit

Servings: 10
Cooking Time: 2 Hours

Ingredients:

- 2-3 cups garlic cloves Enough to cover the bottom of the slow cooker. Use pre-peeled garlic cloves for ease. I used two 6-oz. packages of garlic cloves.
- 1 1/2 cups olive oil can use extra virgin olive oil
- 1 1/2 tsp. salt
- 1/2 tsp. ground black pepper
- 1/2 tsp. red chili flakes
- 8+ springs fresh thyme or 1 tsp. dried thyme

Directions:

1. Add the garlic to the slow cooker.
2. Sprinkle over the salt, pepper and red chili flakes.
3. Lay over the thyme sprigs.
4. Pour over the olive oil.

5. Cover and cook on HIGH For 2 hours without opening the lid during the cooking time.
6. Spread the warm garlic cloves on sliced baguette, or use in your favorite recipes.
7. Botulism Warning! Garlic confit must be stored properly. After serving, promptly refrigerate. Do not leave out on the counter. Use within 3 days or freeze. This is NOT a canning recipe.

NOTES

How to store properly (very important)

If leftover garlic confit is stored improperly (at room temperature or warm temperatures or kept too long), it can produce a botulism toxin.

To prevent this, eat immediately. Or after cooking, place in the fridge and only keep for three days. Do not use it if you forget it out on the counter.

Do not attempt to can this recipe.

How to use:

Appetizer - Slice a fresh baguette and serve the warm (or cold) garlic confit with it. Let your guests use a small knife to spread the garlic cloves on their sourdough bread.

Use in this - the oil is excellent in salad dressings, pasta dishes, or for sauteeing vegetables. The garlic cloves can be used in slow cooker meals like roasted garlic beef sandwiches, mashed potatoes, or even spread on a sandwich instead of mayo.

Can I use vegetable oil?

You can use vegetable oil or canola oil if you choose! You will still have great-tasting garlic confit with just about any oil. Just don't use an intensely flavored oil such as sesame oil.

Can I use different herbs?

Yes, you can use basil, bay leaves, rosemary, or your favorite herbs! You can use fresh herbs or dried herbs.

How do I know if my garlic confit is done?

The garlic cloves will be lightly browned and softened. Do not overcook, for you may end up with a burnt flavored dish.

Slow-cooker Corn Dip

Servings: 6

Ingredients:

- 1 pound frozen corn kernels, thawed
- 8 ounces cream cheese, cubed
- 1/2 cup chopped jarred pimientos
- 2 jalapeños, seeded and finely chopped
- 1 clove garlic, finely chopped
- 1 teaspoon chili powder
- Kosher salt
- 1/4 cup chopped fresh cilantro
- Tortilla chips, for serving

Directions:

1. Special equipment: a slow cooker
2. Combine the corn, cream cheese, pimientos, jalapeños, garlic, chili powder and some salt in a slow cooker. Cook on low heat for 1 hour. Stir to mix in the cream cheese. Continue to cook for another 2 hours. Stir in the cilantro and season with salt.
3. Serve warm with tortilla chips for dipping.

Slow Cooker Black Bean Chilli

Servings: 4

Ingredients:

- 2 tbsp olive oil
- 1 cinnamon stick
- 2 bay leaves
- 1 large red onion, ½ finely chopped, ½ thinly sliced
- 2 sticks celery, finely diced
- 1 green pepper, finely diced
- 3 cloves garlic, finely sliced
- 2 limes, ½ juiced, rest cut into wedges
- 400g tin chopped tomatoes
- 1 tsp smoked paprika, (use hot or sweet depending on your taste)
- 1 tsp cumin seeds, toasted and ground
- 2-3 tsp chipotle chilli paste
- 2 x 400g tins black beans, rinsed and drained

- soured cream to serve
- a small bunch coriander, roughly chopped
- soft corn tortillas to serve
- chilli sauce, to serve, (jalapeño or habanero are good)

Directions:

1. Heat the slow cooker to high or low, depending on desired cooking time.
2. Heat the olive oil in a pan over a medium heat and fry the cinnamon, bay leaves, finely chopped onion, celery, green pepper and garlic for 10 minutes until the veg is soft, turning golden and smelling fragrant.
3. Meanwhile, put the sliced onion in a small pan, cover with boiling water and simmer for 1 minute, drain well and add a pinch of salt and the juice of ½ the lime.
4. Add the tinned tomatoes, ground spices and chipotle paste to the softened vegetables in the pan and bring to the boil. Add the beans, mixing thoroughly, then tip into the slow cooker.
5. Season and cook for 1-2 hours on high or 4-6 hours on low until the beans have absorbed all the flavours and the sauce is rich. Check the seasoning, adding more salt and chilli to taste.
6. Serve the tortillas topped with the beans, soured cream, pickled red onions, coriander and remaining lime wedges.

Slow Cooker Texas Trash Beef And Bean Dip

Servings: 8
Cooking Time: 2 Hours

Ingredients:

- 1 lb. ground beef
- 16 oz. can refried beans (refried pinto or refried black beans)
- 8 oz. pkg. Colby Jack cheese, shredded and divided
- 7 oz. can fire-roasted green chiles, drained
- 8 oz. pkg. cream cheese, room temperature (or microwave for 30 seconds to soften)
- 1 cup sour cream plus more for serving
- 1 oz. pkg. taco seasoning

- Chips for serving
- Optional: Serve with extra sour cream olives and salsa

Directions:

1. Brown meat on the stove-top in a medium sized skillet, or in the slow cooker if your slow cooker has a browning option. Drain the grease. Add meat to slow cooker if using a skillet.
2. Add the refried beans, 2/3 of the cheese, chiles, cream cheese, sour cream and taco seasoning. Stir everything together and flatten out with a spatula. Wipe down edges of slow cooker for a neat appearance.
3. Sprinkle over remaining cheese.
4. Cover and cook on HIGH for 2 hours without opening the lid during the cooking time.
5. Serve with chips and additional sour cream, olives and salsa if desired.

NOTES

Can I skip adding the ground beef?
Yes, this Texas Trash Dip is often served without ground beef. Without the meat, you have an excellent vegetarian meal.
Can I use chicken instead of beef?
Yes, chicken will work great in this dip. Add 2 cups of cooked diced chicken; rotisserie chicken works well.
Can I bake this instead of slow cooking?
You can bake the dip at 350° degrees Fahrenheit for 30 minutes or until hot and bubbly. Serve immediately with chips.

Slow Cooker Union Square Cafe Bar Nuts

Servings: 20
Cooking Time: 1 Hours 20 Minutes

Ingredients:

- 2 lbs. roasted salted mixed nuts
- 6 Tbsp. salted butter
- 1/4 tsp. cayenne pepper
- 2 Tbsp. fresh rosemary, chopped
- 2 Tbsp. brown sugar

Directions:

1. Melt the butter in a small saucepan on the stove top, add the brown sugar, cayenne and rosemary. Stir. No salt is nessesarry unless you have unsalted nuts.
2. Add the mixed nuts to the slow cooker. Pour over the butter mixture. Stir.
3. Cover and cook on HIGH for 1 hour 20 minutes. Stirring every 20 minutes to prevent burning.
4. Serve warm or at room temperature. Enjoy! I found it's better to turn the slow cooker to off while serving these, even the warm function will over cook these and may cause burning.

NOTES

Slow Cooker Size: 4 quart or larger.

The nut mixture I use has brazil nuts, cashews, pecans, macadamia and almonds. Use your favorite mix or single nut.

Sesame seeds are a great addition to this recipe and make it different than most bar nuts.

Slow Cooker Cheese Fondue

Servings: 8

Ingredients:

*   16 oz. block sharp cheddar cheese shredded (don't use preshredded cheese, from the block melts better)
*   2 Tbsp. cornstarch
*   8 oz. cream cheese softened - If you forget to soften, microwave for 30 seconds.
*   2 garlic cloves minced
*   1/2 cup milk
*   For serving:
*   French Bread for serving
*   sliced apples

Directions:

1. Spray the slow cooker with non-stick spray.
2. Add the cheese to the slow cooker and add the cornstarch. Toss the cornstarch with the cheese with clean, dry hands.
3. Add the softened cream cheese, garlic and milk, mix as well as you can. You can mix it more as it heats up.
4. Cook on low for 1 - 1.5 hours, stirring occasionally.
5. Serve with cubed bread and apples.

NOTES

It's important to let leftover cheese fondue cool to room temperature before placing it in the fridge. Pour it into an airtight container and it should keep for up to 4 days. It can even be frozen for up to 2 months.

Other cheeses such as swiss, white cheddar or pepperjack can be used.

If you forget to soften the cream cheese, simply microwave for 30 seconds. That should do the trick!

How To Make Guacamole

Servings: 8

Ingredients:

*   1 large ripe tomato
*   3 avocados, very ripe but not bruised
*   juice 1 large lime
*   handful coriander, leaves and stalks chopped, plus a few leaves, roughly chopped, to serve
*   1 small red onion, finely chopped
*   1 chilli, red or green, deseeded and finely chopped
*   tortilla chips, to serve

Directions:

1. Use a large knife to pulverise 1 large ripe tomato to a pulp on a board, then tip into a bowl.
2. Halve and stone the 3 avocados (saving a stone) and use a spoon to scoop out the flesh into the bowl with the tomato.
3. Tip the juice of 1 large lime, a handful of roughly chopped coriander, 1 finely chopped small red onion and 1 deseeded and finely chopped red or green chilli into the bowl, then season with salt and pepper.
4. Use a whisk to roughly mash everything together. If not serving straight away, sit a stone in the guacamole (this helps to stop it going brown), cover with cling film and chill until needed.
5. RECIPE TIPS
6. EASY CANAPé
7. Wrap finger-size slices of avocado in smoked salmon to serve as a canapé.

Slow Cooker Apple Butter Meatballs

Servings: 10

Ingredients:

- 12 oz. bottle chili sauce (I use Heinz Chili Sauce) Do not use sriracha hot chili sauce or Thai sweet chili sauce.
- 1 1/2 cups apple butter I use Musselman's Apple Butter
- 1 cup pure maple syrup
- 1 Tbsp. molasses
- 1/4 tsp. ground cloves
- 1/4 teaspoon ground cinnamon (or allspice if you have it)
- 40 oz. frozen meatballs (these are precooked and frozen) two 20-ounce bags

Directions:

1. Add the chili sauce, apple butter, maple syrup, molasses, ground cloves, and ground cinnamon to the slow cooker. Stir to combine.
2. Add frozen meatballs to the prepared sauce. Toss to coat.
3. Cover and cook on HIGH for 2.5-3 hours or LOW for 4-5 hours. Stirring occasionally so the meatballs won't burn on the edges. Serve as an appetizer or as an entrée over mashed potatoes or rice with roasted veggies.

NOTES

Where can I find chili sauce?

You can find chili sauce at the grocery store near the ketchup, and the brand is usually Heinz. Do not buy sriracha hot chili sauce or Thai sweet chili sauce.

Where can I find apple butter?

Apple butter is found in the grocery store near the jams and jellies.

Other jams or sauces you can use:

Pumpkin Butter Meatballs - Use one cup of pumpkin butter in place of the apple butter.

Cranberry Meatballs - A can of jellied cranberry sauce is wonderful in this reicpe instead of the apple butter.

Red Current Jelly - Red current jelly has such a tart and wonderful flavor and is great in this recipe. Use one cup instead of the apple butter.

How to store:

Store meatballs in an airtight container within the refrigerator for up to 3 days or in the freezer for up to 3 months.

Slow Cooker Cranberry Meatballs

Servings: 12
Cooking Time: 6 Hours

Ingredients:

- 32 oz frozen meatballs (these are fully cooked, but frozen)
- 28 oz. whole cranberry sauce (two 14-oz. cans)
- 1 cup ketchup
- ¼ cup brown sugar
- 1 Tbsp. lemon juice

Directions:

1. Pour the meatballs into the crockpot.
2. Add the cranberry sauce, ketchup, brown sugar, and lemon juice – stir to combine.
3. Cover and cook on low for 6 hours, stirring occasionally.

NOTES

We serve this as an appetizer with an assortment of cheeses (like brie, cheddar, etc), walnuts, pecans, olives, etc.

If stored properly in an airtight container and refrigerator, these meatballs will keep for up to 4 days.

You can use Heinz chili sauce in place of of the ketchup, in fact they have similar flavors and Heinz chili sauce is not spicy.

The long cooking time ensure the sauce soaks into the meatballs and they will have much more flavor than just cooking them until done.

Slow Cooker Spicy Sausage Dip Recipe

Servings: 8
Cooking Time: 2 Hours

Ingredients:
- 1 lb. hot Jimmy Dean sausage browned and drained
- 16 oz. Mexican sour cream (regular sour cream works too)
- 8 oz cream cheese
- 2 cups Colby-Jack cheese shredded
- 1/4 cup green onion sliced
- 1 jalapeño minced (keep the seeds in if you want it really hot)
- 1 cup salsa I used Newman's medium salsa
- For Serving
- green onion optional garnish
- chips

Directions:
1. Add everything to the slow cooker. Stir everything together, it's ok if some chunks of cream cheese are still there, they will melt in.
2. Stir everything together, some chunks of cream cheese will remain; it'll melt in.
3. Cover and cook on HIGH for 2 hours.
4. When the cooking time is done, stir.
5. Add additional green onions, if desired.
6. Serve with tortilla chips and enjoy!

NOTES

Can I make a double batch?

Yes! A double batch of this sausage cream cheese dip in a 6-quart slow cooker, and you'll have plenty for a large crowd.

Can I use ground beef?

Ground beef works excellent in the creamy dip! Be sure to season it well with salt, pepper, and garlic powder, for it won't have as much flavor as the sausage.

Slow Cooker Beer Meatballs

Servings: 9
Cooking Time: 5 Hours

Ingredients:
- 32 oz. frozen meatballs (26 -32 oz. bag works)
- 2 cups ketchup
- 1 oz. packet Lipton Onion Soup Mix
- 1/2 cup beer

Directions:
1. Add the frozen meatballs to your slow cooker.
2. Pour over the ketchup, onion soup mix and beer. Stir.
3. Cook on low for 5 hours or HIGH for 2.5 hours. Stirring occasionally.

NOTES

Store any leftover meatballs in an airtight container and store them in the fridge for up to 5 days. These can also be frozen for up to 3 months.

To make these barbecue beer meatballs, exchange the ketchup for barbecue sauce!

Sweet And Sour Dhal

Servings: 6
Cooking Time: 2hours 30 Minutes

Ingredients:
- 500 g chana dal lentils
- 50 g butter
- 1 onion, finely chopped
- 1 tsp. dried chilli flakes
- 2 tbsp. dried curry leaves
- 1 tbsp. garam masala
- 3 garlic cloves, crushed
- 3 star anise
- 3 tbsp. tamarind paste
- 3 tbsp. dark muscovado sugar
- 4 large tomatoes, roughly chopped
- Juice 2 limes, plus extra wedges, to serve
- FOR THE BOMBAY PUFFED RICE (OPTIONAL)
- 25 g puffed rice
- 1 tsp. garam masala
- 2 tbsp. tamarind paste

- 1 tbsp. dark muscovado sugar
- 2 tomatoes, finely chopped
- Juice 2 limes
- Handful coriander, roughly chopped
- 1/2 red onion, finely chopped

Directions:

1. In a bowl, rinse the lentils in 3 changes of water. Pour over enough water to cover, then leave to soak for 30min.
2. In a large casserole, heat the butter and fry the onion for 8-10min. Add the chilli flakes, mustard seeds, curry leaves, garam masala and garlic and heat for 1min until the spices release their aroma.
3. Drain the lentils, put into the casserole, and add enough water to cover generously (about 1 litre/1¾ pint). Add the star anise. Bring up to a simmer, turn down and cover the pan, cook over a very low heat so it is barely simmering for 2hr, stirring occasionally. Remove the star anise.
4. Stir in the tamarind paste, sugar, tomatoes and lime juice. Simmer for 15min, or until the tomatoes have broken down. Remove from heat and stand for 5min.
5. If making the Bombay puffed rice, toast the rice in large dry frying pan. Remove from heat and stir in the remaining ingredients. Serve sprinkled on the dhal.
6. For a vegan alternative, swap the butter for 2tbsp sunflower or vegetable oil.
7. IN A SLOW COOKER Soak and drain lentils as in step 1. Complete step 2 in a frying pan; transfer buttery onion mixture to the slow cooker. Add the remaining dhal ingredients, but add only 600ml (1 pint) water. Cook on low for 8-10hr or high for 6hr.
8. GET AHEAD Make dhal (without garnish) up to 2 days ahead, cool and store in the fridge. Reheat slowly on the hob over a low heat until piping hot, stirring often and adding a splash of water, if needed. Garnish with puffed rice, if you like, to serve.

Potato And Fennel 'bake'

Servings: 4
Cooking Time: 3 Hours 50 Minutes

Ingredients:

- 1 small fennel bulb
- 1 leek, trimmed, thinly sliced
- 2 large garlic cloves, very finely chopped
- 1kg coliban potatoes, very thinly sliced
- 100g (1 cup) pre-grated 3 cheese blend
- 300ml Bulla Cooking Cream
- 40g (1⁄2 cup) finely grated parmesan
- 1 small red onion, thinly sliced into rounds
- 1/4 cup small fresh parsley leaves

Directions:

1. Trim the fronds from the fennel and reserve. Thinly slice the fennel and transfer to a bowl. Add the leek and garlic. Toss to combine.
2. Lightly grease the bowl of a 5.5L slow cooker and line with baking paper. Arrange one - third of the potato, overlapping slightly, in the base of the prepared slow cooker. Sprinkle with one - third of the fennel mixture and one - third of the cheese blend. Drizzle with one - third of the cream. Season.
3. Repeat layering the remaining potato, fennel mixture, cheese blend and cream. Cover and cook on High for 3 hours 30 minutes or until the potato is tender. Sprinkle with the parmesan, cover and cook for a further 20 minutes or until cheese has melted.
4. Repeat layering the remaining potato, fennel mixture, cheese blend and cream. Cover and cook on High for 3 hours 30 minutes or until the potato is tender. Sprinkle with the parmesan, cover and cook for a further 20 minutes or until cheese has melted.

Chickpea Dhal With Naans

Servings: 8

Ingredients:

- sunflower oil
- 2 large onions, chopped
- 50g ginger, peeled and grated
- 1 tbsp ground cumin
- 1 tbsp ground coriander
- 1 tbsp nigella seeds, plus more for the naans
- 1 tbsp medium curry powder
- 1 tsp turmeric
- 300g red split lentils
- chana dhal, (dried split chickpeas) 500g
- 2 x 400g tins coconut milk
- NAANS
- 7g fast-action dried yeast
- 100g natural yogurt
- 500g strong white bread flour, plus more for dusting
- 1½ tsp fine salt
- clarified butter or ghee

Directions:

1. To make the naans, mix the yeast and yogurt with 250ml warm water. Put the flour and salt in a bowl and gradually stir in the yeast mixture until it comes together as a dough. Tip out onto the worksurface and knead for 10 minutes, or 5 minutes in a mixer with the dough hook, until smooth. Put into a clean bowl, cover with oiled clingfilm and leave for 2 hours, or until doubled in size.

2. Heat 1 tbsp oil in a large pan, and fry the onion and ginger until really soft. Stir in the spices, cook for 1 minute then add the lentils and chana dhal. Add the coconut milk, 800ml water and some seasoning. Bring to a simmer, turn down to a low heat and cook for 1½ hours, covered, stirring gently every so often, adding more water if needed. To freeze, cool the dhal completely, tip into containers and put in the freezer.

3. When the dough is ready, knead it briefly on a lightly floured worksurface. Cut into 8 pieces and roll each one out to an oval until they no longer spring back. Lay onto oiled baking sheets, cover with oiled clingfilm and leave for 30 minutes until puffy.

4. Heat the oven to 240C/fan 220C/gas 9. Heat another baking sheet in the oven. Transfer the naans, two at a time, onto the hot baking sheet. Cook for 5-10 minutes until the dough starts to bubble and the bottom looks golden. Press them gently back down if they've domed too much. Cool under a clean tea towel, then individually wrap in foil and freeze.

5. To reheat, defrost the dhal in the fridge overnight, and leave the naans on the worksurface to come to room temperature. Heat the oven to 220C/fan 200C/gas 7. Put the dhal into a pan with a splash of water, bring to a simmer and cook until piping hot. Put the naans on a baking sheet, sprinkle with a little water and reheat in the oven for 5 minutes or until warmed through. Brush the naans with clarified butter or ghee, and scatter over some nigella seeds to serve.

VEGETABLES & VEGETARIAN RECIPES

Slow Cooker Green Beans, Ham And Potatoes

Servings: 10

Cooking Time: 2 Hours 45 Minutes

Ingredients:

- 2 pounds fresh green beans, rinsed and trimmed
- 3 ham hocks
- 1 large onion, chopped
- 1 ½ pounds new potatoes, quartered
- 1 tablespoon chicken bouillon granules
- 1 teaspoon garlic powder
- 1 teaspoon onion powder
- 1 teaspoon seasoning salt
- ground black pepper to taste

Directions:

1. Halve green beans if they are large; place in a slow cooker with water to barely cover. Add ham hocks and onion. Cover and cook on High until simmering. Reduce heat to Low; cook until beans are crisp but not done, 2 to 3 hours.
2. Remove ham hocks from the slow cooker. Add potatoes to the slow cooker; cook on Low for 45 minutes.
3. Meanwhile, remove ham meat from the bones, then chop or shred meat and return to the slow cooker. Season with bouillon, garlic powder, onion powder, seasoning salt, and pepper.
4. Use a slotted spoon to transfer green beans, potatoes, and ham into a serving dish with a bit of broth.

Slow Cooker Mushroom Risotto

Servings: 4

Cooking Time: 1 Hours

Ingredients:

- 1 onion, finely chopped
- 1 tsp olive oil
- 250g chestnut mushrooms, sliced
- 1l vegetable stock
- 50g porcini
- 300g wholegrain rice
- small bunch parsley, finely chopped
- grated vegetarian parmesan-style cheese to serve

Directions:

1. Heat the slow cooker if necessary. Fry the onion in the oil in a frying pan with a splash of water for 10 minutes or until it is soft but not coloured. Add the mushroom slices and stir them around until they start to soften and release their juices.
2. Meanwhile pour the stock into a saucepan and add the porcini, bring to a simmer and then leave to soak. Tip the onions and mushrooms into the slow cooker and add the rice, stir it in well. Pour over the stock and porcini leaving any bits of sediment in the saucepan (or pour the mixture through a fine sieve).
3. Cook on High for 3 hours, stirring halfway. and then check the consistency – the rice should be cooked. If it needs a little more liquid stir in a splash of stock. Stir in the parsley and season. Serve with the parmesan.

Crunchy Lemon-pesto Garden Salad

Servings: 6

Ingredients:

- 5 tablespoons prepared pesto
- 1 tablespoon lemon juice
- 2 teaspoons grated lemon zest
- 1-1/2 teaspoons Dijon mustard
- 1/4 teaspoon garlic salt
- 1/4 teaspoon pepper
- 2-1/2 cups thinly sliced yellow summer squash
- 1-3/4 cups thinly sliced mini cucumbers
- 3/4 cup fresh peas
- 1/2 cup shredded Parmesan cheese
- 1/4 cup thinly sliced green onions
- 5 thick-sliced bacon strips, cooked and crumbled

Directions:

1. In a bowl, whisk together the first 6 Ingredients:
2. until blended. In another bowl, combine squash, cucumbers, peas, Parmesan and green onions. Pour dressing over salad; toss to coat. Top with bacon to serve.

Paneer Korma

Servings: 4
Cooking Time: 25 Minutes

Ingredients:

- 3 tbsp vegetable oil
- 225g block of paneer, cut into 2cm cubes
- 1 large onion, roughly chopped
- thumb-sized piece of ginger, peeled
- 2 large garlic cloves
- 5 tbsp korma paste
- 3 cardamom pods, crushed
- 70g ground almonds
- 500ml vegetable stock
- 150g spinach
- 100g Greek yogurt
- rice or naan breads, to serve (optional)

Directions:

1. Heat 1 tbsp of the oil in a deep frying pan over a medium-high heat. Add the paneer cubes and fry for 5 mins, turning regularly, so each side is golden brown. Remove with tongs and put on a plate lined with kitchen paper.
2. Put the onion, ginger and garlic in a food processor with a splash of water and blitz until completely smooth. Heat the remaining oil in the frying pan over a medium-low heat. Add the onion mixture and a pinch of salt, and fry for 10 mins or until lightly golden. Add the korma paste and cardamom, and fry for 1 min. Stir in the ground almonds and fry for 1 min to make a thick paste.
3. Add the stock, bring to a simmer and cook for 5-10 mins, uncovered, or until reduced a little. Add the spinach to the sauce and cook for 5 mins. Stir through the yogurt and paneer, and season generously. Serve with rice or warm naan breads.
4. RECIPE TIPS
5. MAKE IT VEGAN
6. Use firm tofu instead of paneer and swap the yogurt for dairy- free coconut yogurt.

Slow Cooker Baked Potatoes

Servings:
Cooking Time: 4 Hours 30 Minutes

Ingredients:

- 4 baking potatoes, well scrubbed
- 1 tablespoon extra virgin olive oil
- kosher salt to taste
- 4 sheets aluminum foil

Directions:

1. Prick potatoes with a fork several times, then rub with olive oil and season with salt. Wrap tightly in foil and place into the slow cooker.

2. Cook until tender, on Low for 7 1/2 hours or on High for 4 1/2 to 5 hours.

Slow Cooker Stuffed Peppers Recipe

Servings: 3

Cooking Time: 3 Hours 30 Minutes

Ingredients:

- 1 tbsp olive oil
- 1 red onion, peeled and chopped
- 250g chestnut mushrooms, chopped
- 75g shredded kale
- 180g pack chestnuts
- 75g feta, crumbled
- large pinch dried oregano
- 4 large red peppers
- For the pesto
- 50g watercress
- 30g walnut pieces
- 25g hazelnuts
- 100ml extra-virgin olive oil
- ½ lemon, juiced

Directions:

1. In a large frying pan, heat the oil over a medium heat and cook the onion for 3-4 mins, until softened. Add the mushrooms and cook for another 4-5 mins, until softened. Stir in the kale and stir-fry for 1 min, or until starting to wilt.

2. Remove the pan from the heat and add the chestnuts, mashing in the pan using a fork.

3. Sprinkle over the crumbled feta, oregano and mix together well. Season to taste.

4. Slice the tops of the peppers, set aside. Seed the peppers, then divide the mushroom and chestnut mixture equally between them, pressing down into the cavity.

5. Stand the peppers in the dish of a slow cooker and replace the tops. Set the slow cooker to low and cook for 5-5½ hrs, until the peppers are soft.

6. Meanwhile, make the pesto: in the small bowl of a food processor, blitz the watercress with the nuts, until the nuts are broken down. Add the olive oil and lemon juice, season, then process again until nearly smooth. Add a little water if you prefer a looser consistency. Serve the peppers with a drizzle of pesto.

7. Tip: The stuffing can be made in advance and stored in the fridge.

Garden Vegetable Gnocchi

Servings: 4

Ingredients:

- 2 medium yellow summer squash, sliced
- 1 medium sweet red pepper, chopped
- 8 ounces sliced fresh mushrooms
- 1 tablespoon olive oil
- 1/4 teaspoon salt
- 1/4 teaspoon pepper
- 1 package (16 ounces) potato gnocchi
- 1/2 cup Alfredo sauce
- 1/4 cup prepared pesto
- Chopped fresh basil, optional

Directions:

1. Preheat oven to 450°. In a greased 15x10x1-in. baking pan, toss vegetables with oil, salt and pepper. Roast 18-22 minutes or until tender, stirring once.

2. Meanwhile, in a large saucepan, cook gnocchi according to package Directions. Drain and return to pan.

3. Stir in roasted vegetables, Alfredo sauce and pesto. If desired, sprinkle with basil.

Slow Cooker Cheesy Bacon Ranch Potatoes

Servings: 8

Ingredients:

- 6 slices bacon
- 3 pounds red potatoes, chopped
- 1 1/2 cups shredded cheddar cheese, divided
- 1 tablespoon Ranch Seasoning and Salad Dressing Mix, or more, to taste
- 2 tablespoons chopped chives

Directions:

1. Preheat oven to 400 degrees. Line a baking sheet with aluminum foil.
2. Spread bacon in a single layer onto the prepared baking sheet. Place into oven and bake until brown and crispy, about 12-14 minutes. Let cool before crumbling; set aside.
3. Line a slow cooker with aluminum foil, leaving enough to overhang to wrap the potatoes on top, and coat with nonstick spray. Place a layer of potatoes evenly into the slow cooker. Top with cheese, Ranch Seasoning and bacon, repeating 2 more times and reserving 1/2 cup cheese.
4. Cover potatoes with aluminum foil. Cover and cook on low heat for 7-8 hours or high heat for 3-4 hours, or until potatoes are tender. Sprinkle with remaining 1/2 cup cheese. Cover and cook until melted, about 1-2 minutes.
5. Serve immediately, garnished with c

Slow Cooker Lasagne

Servings: 4-6

Cooking Time: 6 Hours 25 Minutes

Ingredients:

- 2 tsp. vegetable oil
- 1 onion, finely sliced
- 2 garlic cloves, crushed
- 1 tsp. dried oregano
- 1 tsp. dried basil
- 400 g beef mince
- 675 g passata
- 1 tsp. sugar
- 1 beef stock cube, crumbled
- 6 x fresh lasagne sheets, torn to size
- 500 g bechamel or cheese sauce, we used Waitrose Cook's Ingredients
- 75 g Cheddar, grated

Directions:

1. Heat the oil in a large pan over medium heat. Add the onion and a pinch of salt and cook for 10min, until softened. Stir in the garlic and dried herbs and cook for 1min, until fragrant. Increase heat to high and add the mince, stirring occasionally, until browned all over, about 10min.
2. Stir in the passata, sugar, stock cube and some seasoning, mixing until the stock cube dissolves. Remove pan from heat.
3. To assemble, spread 1/3 of the beef mixture in the base of the slow cooker bowl, then lay over 1/3 of the pasta sheets in a single layer to cover. Top with 1/3 of the bechamel or cheese sauce. Repeat layering twice more, ending with the bechamel or cheese sauce. Sprinkle over the Cheddar, cover and cook on low for 6hr.
4. Serve with a crisp green salad, if you like.

Slow-cooker Vegan Baked Beans

Servings: 8
Cooking Time: 9 Hours

Ingredients:
- 1 pound dried navy beans
- 2 cups water
- 1 medium onion, chopped
- 1/2 cup molasses
- 1/3 cup packed brown sugar
- 2 tablespoons ketchup
- 2 teaspoons ground mustard
- 1/2 teaspoon liquid smoke, optional
- 1/2 teaspoon salt
- 1/2 teaspoon pepper
- 1/4 teaspoon ground nutmeg
- 1/4 teaspoon ground cloves

Directions:
1. Sort beans and rinse in cold water. Place beans in a large bowl; add enough water to cover by 2 in. Let stand, covered, overnight.
2. Drain and rinse beans, discarding liquid. Transfer beans to a greased 3-qt. slow cooker. In a small bowl, combine remaining 11 Ingredients:
3. . Stir into slow cooker.
4. Cook, covered, on low 9-10 hours or until beans are tender.

Slow-cooked Tomatoes With Basil

Cooking Time: 3 Hours-4 Hours

Ingredients:
- 3kg small tomatoes, from the vine, halved
- 4 tsp herbes de Provence
- large bunch basil, leaves only
- 500ml light olive oil, plus extra for drizzling
- 2 tsp black peppercorn

Directions:
1. Heat oven to 140C/fan 120C/gas Spread the tomato halves over 2 large baking trays, cut-side up. Season with salt and pepper, scatter with the herbes de Provence and drizzle with a little olive oil. Roast in the oven for about 3-4 hrs, or until semi-dried and intensely red. They should be dry in the middle and have a chewy texture – the best way to test is to try one. Place a small basil leaf or piece of torn basil on top of each tomato half for the final hour of cooking.
2. Heat the oil and peppercorns in a saucepan. Pack into jars or heatproof containers (as before) and cover with the oil. Keep in the fridge for up to 1 week.

Slow-cooker Greens And Dumplings

Servings: 4-6

Ingredients:
- 1 1/2 pounds collard greens, chopped
- 1 1/2 pounds kale, chopped
- 1 pound thick-cut pancetta, diced
- 3 cups chicken stock
- One 15.5-ounce can cannellini beans, drained and rinsed

- 2 tablespoons apple cider vinegar
- 1 tablespoon brown sugar
- A few shakes hot sauce, such as Tabasco
- 1/2 teaspoon kosher salt
- Freshly ground black pepper
- 2 cloves garlic, minced
- 2 large shallots, finely chopped
- One 11-ounce can French bread dough, sliced into 1/2-inch pieces

Directions:

1. Combine the greens, pancetta, chicken stock, beans, apple cider vinegar, brown sugar, hot sauce, salt, pepper, garlic and shallots in a slow cooker and fold to combine. Top with the bread dough. Cover and cook on high for 4 hours.

Spiced Ginger Beer Slow Cooker Cabbage

Servings: 6
Cooking Time: 6 Hours-8 Hours

Ingredients:

- 1 red cabbage (about 1kg), sliced
- 1 red onion, sliced
- 2 large eating apples, each sliced into six wedges
- thumb-sized piece of ginger, peeled and finely grated
- 50g butter
- 100ml chicken or vegetable stock
- 300ml alcoholic ginger beer
- ½ tbsp light brown soft sugar
- 2 tsp coriander seeds, crushed
- 1 star anise
- 2 tbsp cider vinegar

Directions:

1. Heat the slow cooker to low. Put all the Ingredients in the slow cooker and add a good grinding of black pepper and 1 tsp salt. Stir well, then cook for 5 hrs.

2. Remove the lid, turn the slow cooker to high and cook for a further 1 hr to reduce the liquid slightly. Taste for seasoning and serve in a warmed bowl.

Slow Cooker Coconut Lentil Curry Recipe

Servings: 6
Cooking Time: 4 Hours

Ingredients:

- ½ cups dried brown lentils
- 2 tablespoons ginger, chopped
- 1 tablespoon EACH: cumin, coriander, turmeric
- Optional: 1-2 teaspoons cayenne powder
- 28 ounce can of crushed tomatoes
- 1 head garlic, chopped
- ½ medium onion, finely minced
- 3 cups water
- 15 ounce can coconut milk
- 2-3 teaspoons sea salt
- 1 cup chopped cilantro
- A few handfuls of cherry tomatoes
- Optional: cooked rice for serving

Directions:

1. Add the dried brown lentils, ginger, cumin, coriander, turmeric, if using the cayenne, crushed tomatoes, garlic, onion, and 3 cups of water in your crockpot. Put the lid on and set the timer for 4 hours on high or 8 hours on low.

2. 1 ½ cups dried brown lentils,2 tablespoons ginger,1 tablespoon EACH: cumin, coriander, turmeric,Optional: 1-2 teaspoons cayenne powder,28 ounce can of crushed tomatoes,1 head garlic,½ medium onion,3 cups water

3. Stir the coconut milk, 2 teaspoons of sea salt, cilantro, and cherry tomatoes into the curry. Taste and add extra salt to taste.

4. 15 ounce can coconut milk,1 cup chopped cilantro,A few handfuls of cherry tomatoes

5. Serve on its own or over a bed of rice.

Vegan Slow Cooker Chilli

Servings: 4
Cooking Time: 4 Hours 10 Minutes

Ingredients:

- 2 tsp. vegetable oil
- 1 large onion, finely chopped
- 1/2 -1tbsp hot chilli powder, to taste
- 1 tsp. ground cumin
- 1 tsp. smoked paprika
- 2 garlic cloves, crushed
- 1 tbsp. tomato purée
- 2 celery sticks, finely sliced
- 1 carrot, peeled and chopped
- 1 red pepper, finely sliced
- 1 large sweet potato, peeled and cut into 2cm pieces
- 400 g tin chopped tomatoes
- 400 g tin kidney beans, drained and rinsed
- 400 g tin black eyed beans, drained and rinsed
- 400 ml vegan vegetable stock
- 25 g vegan dark chocolate
- Small handful coriander leaves, roughly chopped (optional)

Directions:

1. Heat oil in a large pan over medium heat, add onion with a large pinch of salt and cook for 10min, stirring regularly, until softened. Stir in the spices, garlic and tomato purée, and cook for 1min, until fragrant. Transfer to a slow cooker.

2. Add the vegetables, tinned tomatoes, beans and stock. Cook on high for 4hr, until the sweet potato

is cooked through. Stir through the dark chocolate until melted, and sprinkle with coriander, if using. Serve with rice and guacamole, if you like.

Slow Cooker Vegetarian Lentil Curry

Servings: 6
Cooking Time: 3 Hours 20 Minutes

Ingredients:

- 2 tbsp olive oil
- 1 brown onion, finely chopped
- 4 garlic cloves, crushed
- 2 1/2 tsp mild curry powder
- 305g (1 1/2 cups) green lentils, rinsed, drained
- 1L (4 cups) Massel Vegetable Liquid Stock
- 400g can diced tomatoes
- 1 large carrot, peeled, cut into 2cm pieces
- 1 large red capsicum, deseeded, cut into 2cm pieces
- 1 long fresh red chilli, thinly sliced
- 270ml can coconut milk
- 200g green beans, trimmed, cut into 4cm pieces
- Steamed basmati rice, to serve
- Fresh coriander leaves, to serve

Directions:

1. Heat the oil in a large frying pan over high heat. (Alternatively, use the Browning function on a slow cooker.) Add onion and garlic and cook, stirring, for 4 minutes or until onion softens. Add curry powder and cook, stirring, for 1 minute or until aromatic. Add lentils and stir until coated.

2. Add stock, tomatoes, carrot, capsicum and half the chilli. Cover and cook on High for 3 hours (or Low for 6 hours) or until lentils and vegetables are tender.

3. Add the coconut milk and beans and stir until combined. Cover and cook on High for a further 15

minutes (or Low for 30 minutes) or until beans are tender. Season. Serve with rice topped with coriander and remaining chilli.

Slow Cooker Vegetable Curry

Servings: 2
Cooking Time: 6 Hours

Ingredients:

- 400ml can light coconut milk
- 3 tbsp mild curry paste
- 2 tsp vegetable bouillon powder
- 1 red chilli, deseeded and sliced
- 1 tbsp finely chopped ginger
- 3 garlic cloves, sliced
- 200g butternut squash (peeled weight), cut into chunks
- 1 red pepper, deseeded and sliced
- 1 small aubergine (about 250g), halved and thickly sliced
- 15g coriander, chopped
- 160g frozen peas, defrosted
- 1 lime, juiced, to taste
- wholemeal flatbread, to serve

Directions:

1. Put the coconut milk, curry paste, bouillon powder, chilli, ginger, garlic, butternut squash, pepper and aubergine into the slow cooker pot and stir well. Cover with the lid and chill overnight.
2. Cook on low for 6 hrs until the vegetables are really tender, then stir in the coriander and defrosted peas. The heat of the curry should be enough to warm them through. Taste and add a good squeeze of lime juice, if you fancy extra zing. Serve with a wholemeal flatbread.
3. RECIPE TIPS
4. ADD SWEET POTATOES

5. You can swap the squash for sweet potatoes if you prefer – they will still count towards one of your five-a-day, unlike white potatoes.

Roast Tomatoes

Servings: 4
Cooking Time: 1 Hours

Ingredients:

- 10 large vine tomatoes, halved
- 4 garlic cloves, sliced
- ½ bunch thyme
- 3 tbsp balsamic vinegar
- 2 tbsp olive oil

Directions:

1. Heat the oven to 160C/140C fan/gas 3. Put the tomatoes on a baking sheet with the garlic and thyme, drizzle over the balsamic vinegar and olive oil. Add some seasoning and roast for 1 hr. Remove and set aside to cool.
2. RECIPE TIPS
3. ROAST TOMATO & WATERCRESS SALAD
4. Divide an 85g bag watercress between 4 plates. Sprinkle over a small bunch of snipped chives, then top with roast tomatoes.
5. Scatter over 50g walnuts, broken into pieces and pour over the tomato juices as a dressing.
6. Serve with crusty bread, if you like.
7. ROAST TOMATO SOUP
8. Tip the roast tomatoes into a pan with 2 grated carrots. Then, pour on 300ml vegetable stock and simmer for 5 mins. Add some seasoning and whizz with a stick blender until smooth.
9. Serve with crusty bread.

Creamy Chickpea And Vegetable Curry

Servings: 6

Cooking Time: 3 Hours 50 Minutes

Ingredients:

- 2 tsp vegetable oil
- 2 tbsp Madras curry paste
- 1 cup Massel vegetable liquid stock
- 400ml can Coles light coconut cream
- 1 large red capsicum, cut into 2cm pieces
- 1kg pumpkin, cut into 2cm pieces
- 1 small cauliflower, trimmed, cut into florets
- 3 tomatoes, roughly chopped
- 300g green beans, trimmed, halved
- 400g can Coles Chickpeas, drained, rinsed
- 1 Lebanese cucumber, grated
- 2 tbsp fresh coriander leaves, chopped, plus extra to serve
- 1 cup plain Greek-style yoghurt (or your choice of dairy-free yoghurt)
- 4 Coles Kitchen plain naan, warmed

Directions:

1. Heat oil in a medium saucepan over medium heat. Add curry paste. Cook, stirring, for 30 seconds or until fragrant. Add stock. Bring to a simmer. Transfer to slow cooker.
2. Add coconut cream, capsicum and pumpkin to slow cooker. Season. Cover. Cook on high for 1 hour 30 minutes (or low for 3 hours). Add cauliflower and tomato. Cook for 15 minutes. Add beans and chickpeas. Cook for a further 30 minutes or until beans are just tender.
3. Combine cucumber, coriander and yoghurt in a bowl. Serve remaining curry with naan bread, yoghurt mixture and extra coriander.

NOTES

Refrigerate leftovers in an airtight container up to 3 days.

Slow Cooker Red Cabbage

Servings: 8

Cooking Time: 4 Hours-5hours

Ingredients:

- 1kg red cabbage
- 2 white onions, chopped
- 4 Granny Smiths apples, peeled, cored and chopped
- zest 1 orange or 2 clementines
- 2 tsp ground mixed spice
- 100g light brown soft sugar
- 3 tbsp cider vinegar
- 200ml dry cider
- 25g butter

Directions:

1. Heat your slow cooker to Low. Peel the outer leaves from the cabbage and discard. Quarter the cabbage, removing the tough stem, then thinly slice. Arrange a layer of the cabbage on the bottom of your slow cooker, then top with some of the onions, apples, zest, mixed spice, sugar and some seasoning. Continue to create layers until you have used up these Ingredients. Season.
2. Pour over the vinegar and cider and dot the butter on top. Cover with a lid and cook for 4-5 hrs until tender. Will keep in the fridge, covered, for up to three days or in the freezer for up to two months. Reheat in a pan or in the microwave.

Slow Cooked Cheesy Potatoes

Servings: 6

Cooking Time: 8 Hours 10 Minutes

Ingredients:

- 4 98% fat-free rindless shortcut bacon rashers diced
- 1 onion diced
- 8 baby potatoes quartered
- 1/2 cup Kraft cheese shredded
- 1/2 tsp salt and pepper
- 1 tbs dried herbs
- 50g butter
- 2 shallots chopped

Directions:

1. Line slow cooker with foil, allow enough to cover the potatoes when finished. Line the base of the foil with non-stick baking paper.
2. Layer half each of the bacon, onions, potatoes and cheese in slow cooker. Season to taste and dot with butter.
3. Repeat layers of bacon, onions, potatoes, cheese and butter.
4. Cover with foil.
5. Cover and cook on low for 10 hours or on auto for 6-8 hours.
6. Sprinkle with diced shallots prior to serving.

NOTES

Use baby potatoes, quartered or halved, depending on size and shallot stems (green part), chopped.

Can be placed in a hot oven uncovered to crisp up a bit more if desired. I have baked these in the oven also at 150C for 90 minutes then open the top of the foil and increase oven temp to 180C for a further 20-30 minutes.

Slow-roast Tomato Tatin

Servings: 6

Cooking Time: 50 Minutes

Ingredients:

- 25g butter
- splash of good olive oil
- 800g medium and small mixed tomato, halved across the middle and seeds roughly scooped out
- 1 tbsp light soft brown sugar
- 1 tbsp red wine vinegar
- 1 tbsp fresh thyme leaves or oregano, plus extra to serve
- 375g block all-butter puff pastry
- plain flour, for dusting

Directions:

1. Heat oven to 220C/200C fan/gas 7. Melt the butter with a splash of olive oil in your widest frying pan. Add the tomatoes, skin-side down, in a single layer (you can do this in 2 batches if they won't all fit) and cook over a low heat until they release their juices. Lift out with a slotted spoon and rearrange in a tart tin (roughly 23cm), skin-side down – cram them in as they will shrink a little and you don't want any gaps. Add the sugar and vinegar to the pan, and cook until the pan juices are reduced and syrupy. Drizzle over the tomatoes in the tin, then scatter with the oregano or thyme and season.
2. Roll the pastry out on a lightly floured surface to a good 25-26cm round. Lay on top of the tomatoes, and tuck the edges down. Use a fork to prick holes all over the pastry – this will help the steam to escape.
3. Sit the tart tin on a flat baking tray and bake for 30 mins or until the pastry is golden brown and crisp. Let the tart sit for 10 mins, then run a knife round the edge to release the pastry. Carefully flip the tart

over onto a serving plate or board and scatter with more herbs to serve.

Slow-roasted Tomato & Gruyère Tart

Servings: 6
Cooking Time: 50 Minutes

Ingredients:

- For the pastry
- 200g plain flour, plus extra for dusting
- 100g butter, cut into small pieces
- 50g grated gruyère (or vegetarian alternative)
- For the filling
- 500g smallish vine tomatoes, halved
- 1 tbsp olive oil
- handful basil leaves, torn
- 3 tbsp pesto (choose a vegetarian one)
- 2 eggs
- 150ml single cream
- 150ml milk
- 100g grated gruyère (or vegetarian alternative)
- handful black olives

Directions:

4. Heat oven to 140C/120C fan/gas Arrange the tomatoes over a baking sheet, cut-sides up. Brush lightly with oil and put a little basil on top of each. Bake for 1½ hrs until tomatoes are semi-dried. Remove from the oven and increase the heat to 190C/170C fan/gas 5.

5. To make the pastry, tip the flour into a food processor with the butter and whizz until the mixture resembles fine breadcrumbs. Add cheese and 2-3 tbsp cold water and pulse until the dough comes together. Turn out onto a lightly floured surface and briefly knead.

6. Roll out the pastry and line a 25cm flan tin, there's no need to trim off the excess at this stage. Line the pastry with greaseproof paper and fill with baking beans. Bake for 15 mins, then remove the paper and beans and continue cooking until crisp and light golden. Using a small, sharp knife, carefully trim off excess pastry.

7. Spread the pesto over the base of the pastry case. Lightly whisk the eggs, then whisk in the cream and milk. Season with salt and pepper, then stir in the grated cheese. Pour into the pastry case and arrange the tomatoes over the top, cut-sides up. Scatter with olives and bake for 25-30 mins until puffed and golden, then leave to cool slightly before serving.

NOTES

FENNEL, RED ONION & CUCUMBER SALAD

Slice ½ cucumber diagonally, then halve the slices. Place in a colander and sprinkle with salt. Leave for 30 mins to drain, then rinse and pat dry. Finely shred 2 fennel bulbs and finely slice 1 red onion. Mix the cucumber, fennel and onion in a bowl. Whisk together 2 tbsp lemon juice, 1 tsp each clear honey and Dijon mustard plus some seasoning, then whisk in 3 tbsp olive oil and dress the salad.

SIMPLE CAESAR SALAD

Mash together 4 anchovies and 1 garlic clove with a little oil from the anchovy tin. Spread over 12 thin slices baguette and bake at 180C/160C fan/gas 4 for 10 mins until crisp. Cut each slice in half. Shred 1 head Cos lettuce into a large bowl, add the anchovy croutons and scatter over 50g grated Parmesan. Whisk together 2 tbsp mayonnaise, 2 tbsp white wine vinegar, 3 tbsp olive oil and 1 tsp Worcestershire sauce. Season and use to dress the salad.

Prawn, Pea & Tomato Curry

Servings: 4

Cooking Time: 15 Minutes

Ingredients:

- 1 tbsp vegetable oil
- 2 onions, halved, each cut into 6 wedges
- 6 ripe tomatoes, each cut into 8 wedges
- large knob of fresh root ginger, chopped
- 6 garlic cloves, roughly chopped
- 3 tbsp curry paste (we used Patak's tikka masala paste)
- 400g shelled raw king prawn
- 250g frozen pea
- small bunch coriander, leaves chopped
- basmati rice or chapatis, to serve

Directions:

1. Heat the oil in frying pan, then fry the onions over a medium heat until soft and beginning to brown, about 5 mins. Meanwhile, reserve 8 of the tomato wedges, then whizz the remainder in a food processor with the ginger and garlic.

2. Add the curry paste to the pan for 30 secs. Stir through the tomato mix and remaining tomato wedges, then bubble over a high heat for 5 mins, stirring so the sauce doesn't catch. Mix in the prawns and peas; simmer until prawns are pink and cooked through. Scatter with coriander, then serve with rice.

NOTES

IF YOU WANT TO USE A SLOW COOKER...

Leave this to simmer away in a slow cooker. Whizz the oil, ginger, garlic, curry paste and all but 8 tomato wedges to a paste. Scrape into your slow cooker and stir in the onions. Cover and cook on High for 3 hours. Mix in the remaining tomato, prawns and peas, then cover and cook for 30 mins-1 hour further until the prawns are cooked, Serve as above.

Miso Eggplant With Pickled Vegetables

Servings: 4

Cooking Time: 4 Hours

Ingredients:

- 1/4 cup white miso paste
- 2 tsp soy sauce
- 2 garlic cloves, crushed
- 1/2 tsp sesame oil
- 2 tbsp mirin seasoning
- 2 tsp caster sugar
- 2 medium eggplant, halved lengthways
- 1 cup sushi rice
- Pickled ginger, to serve
- Green onion, sliced, to serve
- Sesame seeds, toasted, to serve
- Pickled vegetables
- 1 small carrot, cut into thin matchsticks
- 1 small Lebanese cucumber, seeded, cut into thin matchsticks
- 1/3 cup rice wine vinegar
- 2 tsp caster sugar

Directions:

1. Combine miso paste, soy sauce, garlic, oil, mirin, sugar and 2 tablespoons water in a jug. Spoon 2 tablespoons miso mixture into slow cooker, spreading to cover base.

2. Using a sharp knife, score the flesh of the eggplant in a criss-cross pattern, being careful not to cut through the skin. Place in slow cooker, cut-side up. Spoon over remaining miso mixture. Cook on high for 2 hours (or low for 4 hours), basting with miso mixture halfway through cooking.

3. Meanwhile, make Pickled Vegetables; Place carrot, cucumber, vinegar, sugar and 2 tablespoons water

in a bowl. Season with salt and pepper. Cover. Set aside for 2 hours.

4. Just before eggplant is ready, rinse rice under cold water. Cook rice, using absorption Directions, following packet Directions.

5. Drain pickled vegetables. Rinse under cold water. Drain well. Serve eggplant with pickled vegetables, ginger, green onion and rice. Sprinkle with sesame seeds.

NOTES

To make this recipe in the oven:

Follow step 3. Preheat oven to 180C/160C fan-forced. Line a large roasting pan with baking paper. Follow step 1, adding an extra 1 tablespoon of water. Spoon 2 tablespoons miso mixture over base of prepared pan. Follow step 2, placing eggplant and remaining miso mixture in pan. Cover with foil. Bake for 1 hour, basting with miso mixture halfway through cooking. Remove foil. Bake for a further 20 minutes or until eggplant is golden and tender. Follow steps 4 and 5.

Vegetarian Pho

Servings: 4

Cooking Time: 4 Hours 20 Minutes

Ingredients:

- 250g rice vermicelli noodles
- 1 bunch baby pak choy, quartered lengthways
- 300g firm tofu, cut into 1.5cm pieces
- Bean sprouts, to serve
- Fresh Vietnamese mint sprigs, to serve
- Sliced fresh red chilli, to serve
- Hot chilli sauce, to serve
- Lime wedges, to serve
- Vegetable broth

- 2 cinnamon sticks
- 2 whole star anise
- 5 cloves
- 1 1/2 tsp coriander seeds
- 1 tsp black peppercorns
- 1 large brown onion, quartered
- 5cm-piece ginger, peeled, halved horizontally
- 20g (3/4 cup) sliced, dried shiitake mushrooms
- 3L (12 cups) Massel vegetable liquid stock
- Light soy sauce, to taste

Directions:

1. To make the broth, place the cinnamon, star anise, cloves, coriander seeds and peppercorns in a dry frying pan over medium heat. Cook, shaking the pan occasionally, for 2-3 minutes or until aromatic. Set aside to cool slightly. Transfer mixture to a piece of muslin cloth and tie up with kitchen string to make a pouch. Add the onion and ginger to the frying pan and cook, turning often, for 3-5 minutes or until lightly charred.

2. Place the onion mixture, muslin pouch and mushroom in a 6L slow cooker. Add the stock. Cover and cook on High for 4 hours to develop the flavours.

3. Five minutes before the broth is ready, place the noodles in a large heatproof bowl and cover with boiling water. Set aside for 5 minutes to soften. Drain well. Remove spice pouch from broth. Stir in soy sauce, to taste.

4. Add the pak choy and tofu to the slow cooker. Cover. Cook on High for 5-10 minutes or until the pak choy is tender. Divide the noodles and soup among serving bowls. Top with bean sprouts, mint and sliced chilli. Serve with chilli sauce and lime wedges.

OTHER FAVORITE RECIPES

Italian Sausage And Cheesy Tomato Macaroni

Servings: 6
Cooking Time: 4 Hours 25 Minutes

Ingredients:

- 1 tbsp extra virgin olive oil
- 1 brown onion, chopped
- 3 middle bacon rashers, trimmed, chopped
- 420g packet Italian beef and pork sausages
- 1 cup Massel chicken style liquid stock
- 420g can condensed tomato soup
- 3 cups dried pasta curls
- 1/3 cup Bulla Cooking Cream
- 1/2 cup frozen peas
- 1/2 cup fresh basil leaves, firmly packed
- 1 1/2 cups mozzarella, grated
- 1/3 cup panko breadcrumbs, toasted
- 2 bunches broccolini, steamed

Directions:

1. Heat oil in a large frying pan over medium-high heat. Add onion and bacon. Cook, stirring, for 5 minutes or until onion is softened. Squeeze sausages from casings. Add to pan. Cook, breaking up sausage mince with a wooden spoon, for 5 minutes or until browned. Transfer to slow cooker. Add stock, soup and 1 cup water. Cover. Cook on high for 1 hour (or low for 2 hours).

2. Add pasta. Cook on high for 1 hour (or low for 2 hours), stirring halfway through, or until pasta is just tender.

3. Stir in cream, peas and basil. Season with pepper. Sprinkle with mozzarella, then breadcrumbs. Cook on high for 15 minutes or until cheese is melted.

Remove lid. Turn cooker off. Stand for 5 minutes. Serve macaroni with steamed broccolini.

NOTES

Don't have a slow-cooker? Follow these directions for cooking on the stovetop:

Using a large heavybased saucepan, follow step 1. Cover. Bring to the boil. Reduce heat to low. Simmer for 20 minutes, stirring halfway. Add pasta. Cook, covered, stirring occasionally, for 25 minutes or until pasta is just tender. Follow step 3. Cook, covered, for 15 minutes or until cheese is melted. Remove lid. Cook for a further 5 minutes.

Slow Cooker Curried Sausages

Servings: 4
Cooking Time: 6 Hours 10 Minutes

Ingredients:

- 500g thick sausage
- 1 large onion
- 5 potatoes, cubed
- 4 carrots, cut into chunks
- 1 cup frozen peas
- 1 tbs curry powder
- 3 cups Massel* Beef Style Liquid Stock
- 2 tbs cornflour

Directions:

1. Pierce sausages and place them in a saucepan with enough cold water to cover them, bring to the boil and simmer gently for 10 minutes.

2. Drain and cool, then remove skins from sausages. Cut into bite-sized chunks.

3. Add potatoes, carrots, onion, peas and sausages to slow cooker.

4. Add stock and curry powder to slow cooker, cover, cook on low for 6 hours.

5. Add cornflour to slow cooker 30 minutes before serving, allow 20 minutes so sauce can thicken.
6. Serve with rice.

Slow Cooker Deep Dish Pizza

Cooking Time: 2 Hours 30 Minutes

Ingredients:

- 8 ounces bulk Italian sausage
- 1/2 cup diced onion
- 1/2 teaspoon garlic powder
- 1 cup tomato puree
- 1 teaspoon Italian seasoning
- salt and pepper
- 1 pound purchased pizza dough
- 1/2 cup shredded mozzarella cheese
- 2 cups shredded Italian cheese blend
- 10-12 pepperoni slices

Directions:

1. Brown sausage in a medium pan, breaking it apart with a wooden spoon. Once sausage is about halfway cooked, add onion. Cook until sausage is no longer pink and onion is soft.
2. Add garlic powder, tomato puree, and Italian seasoning. Simmer until thickened. Season to taste with salt and pepper.
3. Roll dough out on parchment paper so that it is about 2 inches longer and 2 inches wider than a 6-quart crock pot.
4. Place parchment paper and dough into crock pot. Reshape the dough so that it comes 1 inch up the sides. If there is too much excess parchment paper, trim it some. Be sure to leave enough to lift the pizza out of the crock pot.
5. Sprinkle mozzarella cheese on the dough. Spread sauce over dough.
6. Sprinkle Italian cheese blend on top of sauce. Scatter pepperoni on top.

7. Place several layers of paper towels on top of the Slow Cooker and fit the lid on. Be sure the paper towels are pulled tightly under the lid.
8. Cook on HIGH for 2 1/2 to 3 hours or on LOW for 4 to 6 hours. Be sure to open the Slow Cooker and take a peak shortly before the end of cooking time in case your Slow Cooker runs a little hot. You don't want the bottom of the crust to burn.
9. Lift the parchment paper to remove the pizza from the crock pot. Slice pizza and serve.

Slow Cooker Garlic Parmesan Spaghetti Squash

Servings: 4
Cooking Time: 4 Hours 10 Minutes

Ingredients:

- 1 small (1-2 pound) spaghetti squash
- 6 tablespoons unsalted butter
- 3 cloves garlic, minced
- 1/4 cup heavy cream
- 1/3 cup freshly grated Parmesan
- chopped fresh parsley leaves for garnish
- salt and pepper to taste

Directions:

1. Carefully pierce your spaghetti squash with a sharp knife 6-8 times all around.
2. Place it in the bowl of your slow cooker and cook for 3-4 hours on high or 6-8 hours on low.
3. Once the squash is tender, remove from the slow cooker and allow to cool slightly.
4. Once you can safely handle it, slice lengthwise and scoop out seeds.
5. Using a fork, scrape the flesh to create long strands.
6. Return the flesh to the slow cooker and turn it on low. Add cream, garlic, and butter and stir to combine. Continue to cook on low, stirring occasionally, until thickened and creamy.

7. Add Parmesan and stir to combine. Taste and season with salt and pepper appropriately.
8. Serve immediately topped with additional Parmesan and chopped parsley.

Slow-cooker Pizza

Servings: 4

Ingredients:

- Cooking spray, for slow cooker
- 1 lb. pizza dough
- 1 c. pizza sauce
- 2 c. shredded mozzarella
- 1/2 c. freshly grated Parmesan
- 1/2 c. sliced pepperoni
- 1/2 tsp. Italian seasoning
- pinch of crushed red pepper flakes
- 1 tsp. Freshly chopped parsley, for garnish

Directions:

1. Spray bottom and sides of a large slow cooker with nonstick cooking spray.
2. Press pizza dough into bottom of slow cooker until it reaches all edges and bottom is completely covered. Spoon over pizza sauce and spread, leaving about 1" of dough around edges. Top with cheeses, pepperoni, and spices.
3. Cover slow cooker and cook on low until crust turns golden and cheese is melty, 3 to 4 hours.
4. Remove lid and let cool 5 minutes.
5. Using a spatula, remove pizza from crock pot. Garnish with parsley, then slice and serve.

Indian Butternut Squash Curry

Servings: 4

Cooking Time: 40 Minutes

Ingredients:

- 200g brown basmati rice
- 1 tbsp olive oil
- 1 butternut squash, diced
- 1 red onion, diced
- 2 tbsp mild curry paste
- 300ml vegetable stock
- 4 large tomatoes, roughly chopped
- 400g can chickpeas, rinsed and drained
- 3 tbsp fat-free Greek yogurt
- small handful coriander, chopped
- Method
- Cook the rice in boiling salted water, as per pack instructions. Meanwhile, heat the oil in a large frying pan and cook the butternut squash for 2-3 mins until lightly browned. Add the onion and the curry paste and fry for 3-4 mins more.
- Pour over the stock, then cover and simmer for 15-20 mins, or until the squash is tender. Add the tomatoes and chickpeas, then gently cook for 3-4 mins, until the tomatoes slightly soften.
- Take off the heat and stir through the yogurt and coriander. Serve with the rice and some wholemeal chapattis if you like.

Slow Cooker Macaroni Cheese

Servings: 4

Cooking Time: 1 Hours 30 Minutes

Ingredients:

- 1 l (1 ¾ pint) whole milk, plus extra if needed
- 1/2 tsp english mustard powder
- 250 g (9oz) mature Cheddar, grated
- 50 g (2oz) parmesan

- 100 g (3 ½oz) cream cheese
- 400 g (14oz) macaroni
- 6 bacon rashers (optional)

Directions:

1. Put the milk, all the cheeses, mustard powder, a generous pinch of salt and freshly ground black pepper into a slow cooker. Stir well, then add the macaroni and mix again. Cook on low for 1 1/2- 2 1/2 hours until the pasta is cooked and the sauce is creamy. Stir in a splash of milk if the mixture is a little stiff.

2. Cook bacon, then add before serving (you can use ready-cooked bacon if you prefer).

Slow Cooker Lasagna

Servings: 6

Ingredients:

- Meat Mixture:
- 2 teaspoons olive oil
- 1 medium onion diced
- 2 pounds ground beef
- 1 pound Italian sausage, casing removed
- 3 cloves garlic, finely chopped
- One 28-ounce can diced tomatoes
- One 14.5-ounce can diced tomatoes
- One 6-ounce can tomato paste
- 1 tablespoon minced fresh basil
- 1 tablespoon minced fresh flat-leaf parsley
- 1 teaspoon dried oregano
- 1/2 teaspoon kosher salt
- Freshly ground black pepper
- Cheese Mixture:
- 3 cups ricotta cheese
- 3/4 cup freshly grated Parmesan
- 1/2 cup grated Romano
- 1 tablespoon minced fresh basil

- 1 tablespoon minced fresh flat-leaf parsley
- 1/2 teaspoon kosher salt
- 1/2 teaspoon freshly ground black pepper
- 2 large eggs, beaten
- Lasagna:
- Nonstick cooking spray, for spraying the slow cooker
- 15 uncooked lasagna noodles
- 2 cups grated mozzarella
- Chopped fresh flat-leaf parsley, for garnish

Directions:

1. For the meat mixture: In a large skillet over medium-high heat, add the olive oil and onion and saute for 5 minutes. Add the ground beef, sausage and garlic and cook until brown, 7 to 9 minutes. Add the tomatoes with their juice, tomato paste, basil, parsley, oregano, salt and some pepper and stir. Set aside.

2. For the cheese mixture: In a medium bowl, combine the ricotta, Parmesan, Romano, basil, parsley, salt, pepper and eggs and stir together well.

3. For the lasagna: Spray a 6-quart slow cooker with cooking spray.

4. Spoon in one-quarter of the meat mixture on the bottom and top with 5 lasagna noodles, broken to fit. Add a third of the cheese mixture, then sprinkle with 1/2 cup mozzarella. Repeat this layering twice, starting with the meat mixture and ending with the mozzarella, for 3 layers total.

5. For the fourth layer, top with the remaining meat mixture and remaining 1/2 cup mozzarella. Cover and cook on low for 4 hours. Turn off the heat and allow the lasagna to sit 30 minutes before serving. Sprinkle with chopped parsley.

Pepper, Date And Harissa Tagine

Cooking Time: 3 Hours

Ingredients:

- 2 onions, diced
- 2 sticks celery, thinly sliced
- 3 cloves garlic, sliced
- 1 vegetable stock cube, crumbled
- 2 tsp ground turmeric
- 2 x 400g tins chopped tomatoes, strained over
- a bowl to catch the juices
- 1 lemon, zested and juiced
- 2 tbsp harissa (rose harissa if you can find it)
- 2 tbsp runny honey
- 1 tbsp ground coriander
- 1 tsp ground cinnamon
- 6 peppers (a mix of red, yellow and orange),
- cut into chunks
- 150g pitted dates, cut into thirds
- CRUNCHY SALAD
- 1 bulb shredded fennel, or 1 sliced cucumber
- 150g natural yogurt
- 1/2 lemon, juiced
- a small handful mint, chopped
- TO SERVE
- parsley, mint or coriander, to serve
- couscous, flatbreads and hummus

Directions:

1. Heat the slow cooker to high. Put in the onions, celery, garlic, stock cube and turmeric with 600ml of just-boiled water. Pour in the tomato juice and cook for 1 hour
2. Pour in the strained tomatoes. Stir in the lemon juice, harissa, honey, coriander and cinnamon with 1/2 tsp of salt and plenty of freshly ground black pepper. Mix in the pepper chunks and dates, put the lid back on and cook for another 2 hours or until the peppers are soft.
3. Toss together the salad ingredients and season really well.
4. Ladle the tagine into bowls and scatter with the lemon zest and herbs. Serve with the salad, couscous, flatbreads and spoonfuls of hummus

Slow Cooker Mac And Cheese

Servings: 12
Cooking Time: 3 Hours 15 Minutes

Ingredients:

- 1 (16 ounce) package elbow macaroni
- ½ cup butter
- salt and ground black pepper to taste
- 1 (16 ounce) package shredded Cheddar cheese, divided
- 1 (5 ounce) can evaporated milk
- 2 eggs, well beaten
- 2 cups whole milk
- 1 (10.5 ounce) can condensed Cheddar cheese soup
- 1 pinch paprika, or as desired (Optional)

Directions:

1. Fill a large pot with lightly salted water and bring to a rolling boil. Stir in macaroni and return to a boil. Cook pasta uncovered, stirring occasionally, until tender yet firm to the bite, about 8 minutes. Drain and transfer pasta to a slow cooker.
2. Add butter to pasta and stir until melted; season with salt and pepper. Sprinkle about 1/2 of the Cheddar cheese over pasta and stir.
3. Whisk evaporated milk and eggs together in a bowl until smooth; stir into pasta mixture.
4. Whisk milk and condensed soup together in a bowl until smooth; stir into pasta mixture.

5. Sprinkle remaining cheese over pasta mixture; garnish with paprika.

6. Cook on Low for 3 hours.

7. Serve hot and enjoy!

8. Tips

9. Some slow cookers take less time. Check the edges are not getting too brown after 2 1/2 hours.

10. To bake in a conventional oven, pour pasta mixture into a casserole dish and bake at 350 degrees F (175 degrees C) for 45 minutes to 1 hour.

Classic Pasta E Fagioli

Servings: 6

Cooking Time: 35 Minutes

Ingredients:

- 2 tbsp extra virgin olive oil, plus extra for drizzling
- 1 onion, finely chopped
- 2 celery sticks, finely chopped
- 2 carrots, peeled and finely chopped
- 2 garlic cloves, crushed
- 2 rosemary sprigs
- 2 bay leaves
- 1¼ litres vegetable stock
- 400g can chopped tomatoes
- 2 x 400g cans cannellini beans, drained and rinsed
- 200g small pasta shapes (ditalini or cavatelli work well)
- 200g cavolo nero, stalks removed, roughly torn
- grated parmesan or vegetarian alternative, to serve
- Method
- Heat the oil in a large saucepan over a medium heat and fry the onion, celery and carrots for 10 mins until lightly golden. Add the garlic, rosemary and bay and fry for a minute more.
- Add the stock and chopped tomatoes and bring to a simmer. Tip in the cannellini beans, bring back to a simmer and cook for 5 mins. Roughly mash with a

potato masher to break up some of the beans (or pulse once with a hand blender) – this will thicken the soup slightly. Season well.

- Add the pasta and cavolo nero, then simmer for 4-6 mins more until the pasta and greens are tender. Taste for seasoning, then remove and discard the rosemary sprigs and bay. Serve the soup in warmed bowls with a drizzle more olive oil and a grating of parmesan.

Sweet Potato & Coconut Curry

Servings: 6

Cooking Time: 6 Hours 30 Minutes-8 Hours 30 Minutes

Ingredients:

- 4 tbsp olive oil
- 2 large onions, halved and sliced
- 3 garlic cloves, crushed
- thumb-sized piece root ginger, peeled
- 1 tsp paprika
- ½ tsp cayenne
- 2 red chillies, deseeded and sliced
- 2 red peppers, deseeded and sliced
- 250g red cabbage, shredded
- 1kg sweet potatoes, peeled and chopped into chunks
- 300g passata
- 400ml coconut milk
- 2 tbsp peanut butter
- To serve
- small bunch fresh coriander, chopped
- cooked couscous (or gluten-free alternative)
- Method
- Heat 1 tbsp olive oil in a large non-stick frying pan and add the onion. Fry gently for 10 mins until soft then add the garlic and grate the ginger straight into the pan. Stir in the paprika and the cayenne

and cook for another minute then tip into the slow cooker.

- Return the pan to the heat and add another 1 tbsp oil along with the chilli, red pepper and shredded cabbage. Cook for 4-5 mins then tip into the slow cooker.

- Use the remaining oil to fry the sweet potatoes, you may have to do this in 2 or 3 batches depending on the size of your pan. Cook the sweet potatoes for around 5 mins or just until they start to pick up some colour at the edges then put them in the slow cooker too.

- Pour the passata and the coconut milk over the sweet potatoes, stir to mix everything together and cover the slow cooker with a lid and cook for 6-8hrs or until the sweet potatoes are tender.

- Stir the peanut butter through the curry, season well with salt and pepper and serve with couscous and chopped coriander scattered over the top.

Slow Cooker Spaghetti Squash

Servings: 2

Ingredients:
- 1 spaghetti squash

Directions:
1. Rinse and dry the outside of spaghetti squash, then pierce all over (at least 8 times) with a small paring knife.
2. Place squash in slow cooker and cook on high for 1 1/2 hours per pound of squash, checking about every hour to be sure it is not burning, and rotating if needed. (For example, if your squash is 3 pounds, cook for 4 1/2 hours, etc.)

3. To check squash, quickly press it with your finger. If it dents, then it's good to go! If there is some resistance, check again in 15 minutes.
4. When squash is ready, transfer to a cutting board and let cool slightly before halving. Remove seeds and use a fork to shred into strands. Serve with toppings of your choice.

Easy Pesto Pizza

Servings: 8

Ingredients:
- 1 loaf (1 pound) frozen bread dough, thawed
- 1/2 cup shredded Parmesan cheese, divided
- 1/2 teaspoon dried basil
- 1/2 teaspoon dried oregano
- 1/4 cup prepared pesto
- 1 cup sliced fresh mushrooms
- 1 cup shredded part-skim mozzarella cheese

Directions:
1. Preheat oven to 425°. Place dough on a lightly floured surface; let rest for 10 minutes. Knead in 1/4 cup cheese, basil and the oregano. Roll into a 12-in. circle; place on a greased 14-in. pizza pan. Prick with a fork. Bake 10 minutes.
2. Spread pesto over crust. Sprinkle with mushrooms, mozzarella cheese and the remaining Parmesan cheese. Bake pizza until golden brown, 8-10 minutes longer.

Printed in Great Britain
by Amazon

28960272R00062